MUMFIE'S UNCLE SAMUEL

One friend of Mumfie's wrote in *The Listener* 'I predict for Mumfie a small niche among the immortals.'

This might have turned his head had he not been uncertain what exactly a 'niche' was. In any case, since then he scarcely had a moment to spare; adventures fell thick and fast.

3 abc

Other MUMFIE books

HERE COMES MUMFIE
THE WANDERINGS OF MUMFIE

and published by CAROUSEL BOOKS

Katharine Tozer's

Mumfie's Uncle Samuel

Illustrated by the Author

CAROUSEL BOOKS
A DIVISION OF TRANSWORLD PUBLISHERS LTD

MUMFIE'S UNCLE SAMUEL
A CAROUSEL BOOK 0 552 52058 6

Originally published in Great Britain
by John Murray Ltd.

PRINTING HISTORY
John Murray Edition published 1939
John Murray Edition reprinted four times
Carousel Edition published 1975

This low-priced Carousel book has been completely reset in a type face designed for easy reading, and was printed from new plates. It contains the complete text of the original hard-cover edition.

This book is set in Baskerville 12/13 pt.

Carousel Books are published by Transworld Publishers Ltd.
Century House, Uxbridge Road, Ealing W.5.

Made and printed in Great Britain by
Richard Clay (The Chaucer Press) Ltd, Bungay, Suffolk

FOR
URSULA AND ANTONIO

CHAPTER ONE

'I think . . .' said Mumfie. 'Scarecrow, do listen.'

'What?' Scarecrow lay on his back in the sun, idly puffing at a dandelion clock.

'Wouldn't it be a very good idea if we went to visit my Mama?' Mumfie rolled over. 'Don't you think so, Scarecrow?'

'Well . . . Puff!' Scarecrow blew away the last down. 'Now that Selina's gone to school there doesn't seem to be much doing around here. How would we get there?'

Mumfie held up his hankie to see which way the wind was blowing.

'Humph! East. I could write a letter to East and pin it on to this tree, then we will go away and hide, and as soon as it gets blown away we will know that he has come to fetch it. What time did the dandelion say, Scarecrow?'

'Five o'clock.' Scarecrow pushed his hat off his forehead and squinted up at the sky.

'Tea-time,' announced Mumfie. 'What are you looking at?'

'I was just thinking it was a long time since we had been up There. I wander if much has happened since we left. You'd better write the note as soon as we get in; we don't want it to get too dark for East to notice it.'

'I shall write it after tea,' said Mumfie firmly. 'I always think better when I'm full.'

He picked up his new straw hat and followed Scarecrow through the tall trees towards the house.

'Will this do?' he asked presently, looking up from the letter he was writing to the East wind.

'Mumfie, I'm beginning to wonder if I like doughnuts,' muttered Scarecrow. 'I'm not altogether sure that they agree with me. Read it out and let's see.'

'You shouldn't have eaten so many,' said Mumfie severely. 'Now you've probably indigested yourself. Listen.'

He picked up the letter and began to read out.

Dear Mr. East,

I have decided that it would be a good thing for Scarecrow and me to visit my Mama. If it would not be a bother, could you please blow us up There? We will stand under the tree where I have put this letter. We will wear clothes which is warm but not heavy.

Hoping you are well and can oblige.

Yours hopefully,

MUMFIE

'Is that the right way to end, do you think?'

'I think you should end Yours Truly,' suggested Scarecrow. 'It sounds more dignified. Otherwise it's all right.'

They put on their coats and hats and ran off to the tree, where Scarecrow carefully pinned the letter to a low branch which swayed in the wind.

'Now,' said Scarecrow. 'We'd better go a little way off in case he doesn't want us to watch him open it.'

They went down the hill and hid behind a pine tree from which they could see clearly the white envelope against the dark branch.

'Here he comes!' said Scarecrow presently, as a gust of wind buffeted against them. 'My! but he's blowing hard. I do hope he's in a good temper.'

'He's got it,' called Mumfie delightedly, as the white envelope flapped off the branch and was whirled up into the air. 'Now we'd better go back and stand under the tree. Oh, dear, I do hope he doesn't blow us too hard, so that we get separated. Better hold my hand, Scarecrow.'

They waited under the tree while East raced through

the air, bending the tree-tops, and chasing the clouds in ragged pattern across the evening sky.

They stood for a long time hand-in-hand, gazing up expectantly.

'Humph!' said Scarecrow presently. 'We're still here. I suppose you wrote the letter clearly, Mumfie?'

'I did my best writing.' Mumfie sounded a little nervous. 'Most people can read it.'

He jumped into the air hopefully, but came down again in the ordinary manner.

'Oh, goodness! What's that?' He pointed to a small white speck, that circled slowly down towards them.

'Unless someone else uses the same sort of paper, I should say it was your letter.'

Scarecrow stooped to pick it up.

'Yes, it's yours all right. But look, there is something written on the back.'

In pale blue, blowy writing, they made out the words.

Sorry, too busy. Yours very truly,

East

'Oh!' cried Mumfie. 'Oh, dear, oh, dear. Now what are we going to do?'

'Short of borrowing an aeroplane, I don't know.' Scarecrow frowned. 'I don't take that kindly of East. Look at the way he's blowing everything about except us. I believe he did it on purpose. He always did have the most unreliable temper.'

'I wonder what he likes blowing best,' said Mumfie thoughtfully. 'Scarecrow, do you think if we were to give him a nice lot of coloured balloons, he would blow those away?'

'Sure to,' said Scarecrow. 'But I don't see how his blowing away a lot of our balloons would help.'

'It would if we was tied on to the end of them. If we blewed up a big enough bunch, then p'r'aps he wouldn't notice us underneath them.'

Scarecrow chuckled. 'There's no harm in trying it. Come on!'

They raced back to the house, and up into the playroom, where they found a whole packet of balloons which Selina had given them for Christmas.

'We mustn't let him see us blowing them up. We will do it in here—then when we are ready we will tie ourselves on to the strings and push the bunch out of the window.'

Presently they sat among a pile of gay balloons.

'Oh, dear!' puffed Scarecrow, rather red in the face. 'I wish I hadn't eaten all those doughnuts. Do you think that is enough?'

They collected the balloons and tied them in two large clusters. Then they plaited the ends together, and fastened them firmly round their waists.

'Now,' said Scarecrow. 'You go first, then I'll follow as soon as I've seen that it works.'

'Yes,' said Mumfie, looking out of the window. 'But what will happen if it doesn't? It's rather a long way down to the ground.'

'Oh, that will be all right. Even if they don't go up in the air, the balloons will let us down gently, like a parachute.'

'I suppose you are right.' Mumfie sounded rather doubtful. 'Well, here I goes.'

He pushed his balloons out of the window, and Scarecrow holding on to the back of his coat, carefully scrambled over the sill.

East, racing over the house, saw a lovely clump of shining balloons appearing at the window.

'Ha!' he chuckled to himself. 'This will annoy them. Would I give them a lift, indeed—what do they think

I am—a sort of Omnibus?' He tore down, sweeping the shining globes off the sill and up into the air.

'Poof!' cried Mumfie, feeling rather dizzy.

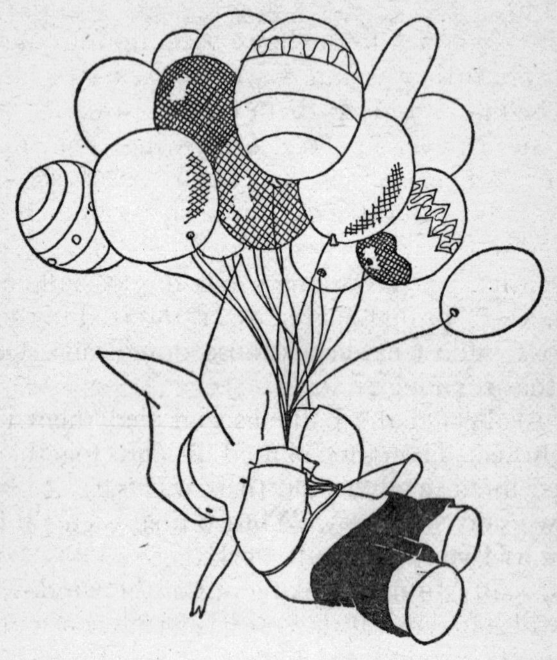

He peeped down to see if Scarecrow were following just as the second bunch floated up out of the window.

They raced away over the park, perilously skimming the tree-tops. Away over the hills, climbing higher and higher, until the earth was lost in dusk below them, and they were surrounded by stars glittering in the pale moonlight.

CHAPTER TWO

Mumfie, who had been dozing comfortably under the balloons, was suddenly awoken by a loud bang just above him.

He looked up sleepily.

'Did you hear something pop?' he called to Scarecrow, who was floating just below him.

But his friend must have been asleep, for there was no reply.

Mumfie was just about to call out again when there was another loud pop, and he suddenly fell a little way through the air.

'Oh, Scarecrow!' he cried in dismay. 'My balloons is popping. Whatever am I to do?—Scarecrow, do wake up!'

But now the balloons were bursting fast, so that he sank gently down, leaving Scarecrow to float about high above him. Mumfie was filled with dismay. He dared not call out very loud for fear of bursting more of the shining rubber balls.

He counted the six remaining ones. If only these would stay up they should carry him along. He looked below him, trying to make out their whereabouts. The morning sun shone down upon a mass of pearly grey clouds.

He descended rapidly towards the clouds, as one after another three more balloons exploded.

'Oh, this is dreadful!—If only Scarecrow would wake up and notice—Scarecrow!' he wailed at the top of his voice.

'Yes,' said Scarecrow drowsily, rubbing the sleep out of his eyes.

'Hey!' He was suddenly wide awake. 'Where are you? Mumfie, where have you got to?'

'Here I am,' came a thin voice from far below him.

He looked down to see Mumfie fast disappearing into a bank of cloud.

'Why, whatever—he's sinking. Now how has he managed that?' Scarecrow gave his balloons a tug, as if to make them fly lower.

'No, that doesn't do it. Gracious—I shall have to think of something quickly, or I shall lose sight of him altogether. Oh, my word—he's out of sight now. Hang on, Mumfie!' he bellowed through his hands. 'I'm coming.'

He pulled down one of the balloons, and tried to undo the knot which tied it.

'No—that's no good, it'll take much too long—I shall have to burst it, though what we'll do if we want to get up again, I don't know. Still—Bang!—there's no time to think about that now—Bang! Bang! Bang! —there, now we're sinking. Still it's a long way to the clouds yet. However many more—Bang!—have I got to—Bang!—burst. Oh, dear, I hope I haven't overdone it. Ugh! it's wet.'

Scarecrow had reached the cloud-belt and was wrapped in soft wet mist. He looked about him for any sign of Mumfie, but it was impossible to see anything.

Lower and lower he sank, calling out from time to

time. Once or twice he thought he heard a faint answering call, but the mist muffled his voice as though he were wrapped in a blanket.

'Well, this is a fine kettle of fish,' he muttered. 'It is to be hoped that we don't land in the sea—that's all I have got to say. Hullo, we're coming out.'

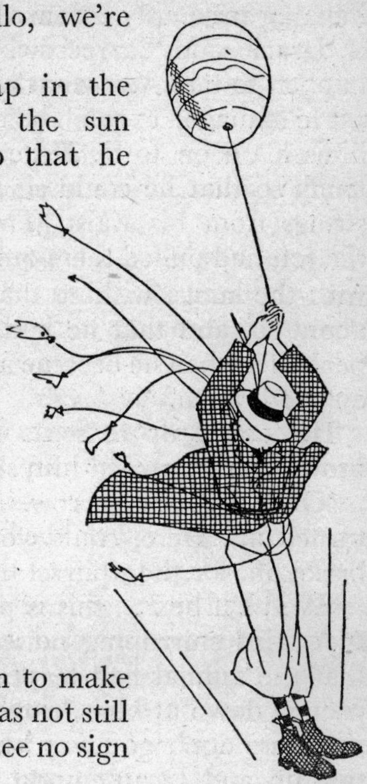

He had reached a gap in the clouds through which the sun filtered, dazzling him so that he found it difficult to see. He shaded his eyes with his hand.

'Oh, my word. Lower than I thought—and all that damp hasn't done my balloons any good—they'll soon start to burst by themselves I shouldn't wonder. Of course I would go and land over a forest. A fine chance I'll have of finding Mumfie among all those trees.'

He looked around again to make sure that his little friend was not still floating about, but could see no sign of him.

'I'd better land myself, there's nothing else for it. This forest seems to go on for miles—Mumfie must be somewhere inside it.'

Scarecrow carefully burst another balloon, and by wriggling about, managed to bring himself over what looked like a small clearing.

'Now for it!' He exploded all the balloons except the last one.

'OO-er!' he breathed as he shot rapidly down. As he fell among the tree-tops he tried frantically to steer clear of the sharp-needled pine-branches. He was managing quite well when the string of the balloon became entangled. A violent jerk, and he was left hanging perilously below a wide branch.

'Drat!' said Scarecrow. 'Things like this always happen to me. *Now* what am I going to do?'

He managed to catch hold of the branch and to drag himself up on to it. He edged his way towards the trunk so that he could sit safely while he untied the strings from his waist. This was rather difficult, as the jolt had pulled them quite tight. He was struggling with the knots, wishing that the tree would not sway about so, and that he had remembered to bring his penknife, when he became aware that he was not alone on the branch.

He looked up to see a red squirrel whose bright brown eyes regarded him shyly.

'Oh,' said Scarecrow. 'Thank goodness you've turned up. Here, could you help me with . . .?' He broke off, for the squirrel had disappeared.

'Well I'll be . . . this is provoking. Hi! Squirrel.'

A faint chirruping noise just above him told him that the animal had leapt on to a higher branch. It peeped down at him through the fir-cones.

'Please don't go away,' begged Scarecrow. 'I'm all tied up and I can't undo myself, and I don't fancy spending the rest of me life up this tree. Besides, all the time I am sitting up here, we are probably getting farther and farther apart,' he added under his breath.

The squirrel hopped farther down the branch as though to look at him more closely.

'I'm quite harmless—really I am,' said Scarecrow pleadingly.

The tight strings round his waist were becoming more and more uncomfortable every moment.

The squirrel seemed to hesitate. Then suddenly appearing to make up its mind, it hopped down on to the lower branch, and came a little way towards him.

'Er—can I be of any assistance?' it asked nervously, in a tiny voice.

'Yes, indeed you can,' replied Scarecrow in the softest voice he could manage. He did not want to frighten the little creature away again.

'If you could just help me to undo this string round my waist, then I could get down on to the ground.'

'Well, I might,' squeaked the squirrel doubtfully, coming a little closer. It stopped just in front of him.

'I don't want to seem inquisitive,' it said, 'but we watched you coming down out of the sky. Are you a bird or something? We've never seen a bird quite like you. I don't wish to seem rude, but Mama always says that it doesn't do to take risks.'

'No, I'm not a bird,' laughed Scarecrow. I'm a

scarecrow, and there's no risk I assure you. I only want to get down out of this tree.'

'Oh, well,' shrilled the squirrel, 'I'll bite you undone. But I'm going to look very silly if it's a trap, like my Uncle Henry up there says it is.'

'It's a trap!' called a voice from above. 'Don't say I didn't warn you.'

'Oh, for goodness' sake—I'm not a trap.' Scarecrow tried not to sound impatient. 'Do hurry up. I can't stand this tightness much longer.'

'Well, I'll risk it,' decided the squirrel. 'If only to show my Uncle Henry he is wrong.'

It began to nibble at the string, and very soon had bitten it through.

'Thank you very much, old fellow,' said Scarecrow, stretching himself, and feeling better now that the tightness was removed from his waist. 'Now you can go and cock snooks at your Uncle Henry. A trap, indeed!' He started to scramble off the branch.

'Are you going now?' asked the squirrel. 'I've often heard the birds talking about scarecrows, but I myself have never seen one before. Now that you are here it's a pity that you should go so soon. I must say, now that I've seen you, you are a bit different from what I should have expected after listening to the birds' description.'

'Humph!' said Scarecrow, a little offended. 'Don't you listen to what *they* say. Birds, indeed! I should like to stay, if only to give you my opinion about birds. But I've got to hurry—I'm looking for a friend of mine who should be down in the wood below.'

'My! My!' The squirrel hopped up and down in what seemed to Scarecrow a perilous manner.

'Another scarecrow! Fancy having two scarecrows in the wood at the same time.'

'Oh, he isn't a scarecrow. As a matter of fact he's a small elephant, he's . . .'

'Oh, you mean Mumfie. Is it Mumfie you are looking for?' asked the squirrel rather surprisingly.

'Well, I'll be blowed!' Scarecrow nearly fell out of the tree with amazement. 'However did you know?'

'We all know Mumfie,' said the little creature in a matter-of-fact voice. 'He used to live in this forest. We have been wondering when he would come back to pay a visit. He's been away a long time. I expect he will find things rather changed around here.'

Scarecrow could hardly get over his surprise at the good fortune which had landed them over Mumfie's wood.

'Which way did he go?' he asked eagerly.

'He came down here, the same as you did—only he made a better landing. He hardly stopped to say how do you do—seemed quite upset about something—said a friend of his was still floating about in the sky. I couldn't make out what he was talking about. But come to think of it, I suppose he was referring to you.'

'You bet he was,' agreed Scarecrow. 'But which way did he go?' he asked again.

'Down through the rhododendron bushes over there—there's another clearing farther on.'

'Thanks.' Scarecrow hurried off.

The squirrel peeped at him from its perch on the branch until he was hidden beyond the bushes, then it ran back into a hole in the tree-trunk.

CHAPTER THREE

'Mumfie!' called Scarecrow as he pushed his way through thick bushes bright with purple and scarlet flowers.

He came out into the clearing just in time to see a small red-coated figure disappearing down an avenue of trees.

'Mumfie!' he bellowed. 'Here I am.' He rushed along, calling as he went.

'Oh, thank goodness,' said Mumfie. 'Scarecrow, all my balloons popped and I started to fall down. I was so afraid you wouldn't notice that I had gone. How did you manage to land?'

Scarecrow told him of his adventures as they went along through the forest.

'I met a squirrel who knew you. Isn't it luck we managed to land right over your forest? It's a good thing that East didn't catch sight of us under the balloons. Is it a long way to your house, Mumfie?'

'I don't think it's very far,' said Mumfie. 'But the forest is so big that one is apt to get muddled. I think this will be the quickest way through. Oh, yes, there's the rowan tree. Come along, Scarecrow. Won't Mama be excited to see us!'

He trotted along, singing a cheerful song to himself, and giving little skips into the air.

The wood was thick with wild flowers: primroses, violets, and star-shaped wood anemones. Mumfie picked some as he went along.

'Look, Scarecrow, what a pretty bunch. I shall give them to Mama. O-o, they do smell lovely.'

He buried his nose in the fragrant nosegay.

'Here we are,' he announced presently. 'This is the clearing. Oh, my, I feels all excited inside.'

He ran forward a little way, and then suddenly stopped.

'I can't see any house,' said Scarecrow.

But Mumfie was staring, his eyes round with dismay.

'Oh, Scarecrow—whatever's happened?' he wailed.

For in the walled-in clearing ahead of them stood no round cottage with its familiar red chimney and blue front door—only the charred, burnt shell of a cottage, with scorched grass, and forlorn, blackened tree stumps around it.

Mumfie ran forward as far as the charred doorframe. Then he sat down and bellowed aloud.

'Please don't cry,' comforted Scarecrow, sitting down beside him, and trying not to sound too anxious. 'Perhaps we've come to the wrong place.'

'No, we hasn't,' sobbed Mumfie. 'Oh! OH! OH!

My poor Mama—her house is all burnt down. Whatever shall I do?'

'There's only one thing to be done,' said Scarecrow in the most cheerful voice he could muster. 'When somebody's house gets burnt down, the best thing to do is to build them a new one.'

Mumfie brightened a little, then his face crumpled up again.

'Yes, but wherever have they gone to?' he sobbed. 'I want my Mama.'

'They've probably gone to stay with relations until their new house is ready,' suggested Scarecrow sensibly. 'Have you any relations living somewhere near here?'

'Well,' said Mumfie doubtfully. 'There's my Uncle Samuel; but he doesn't live very near here—and anyway, I don't think they would go to *him*.'

'At least he would be someone to try. How do we get there?'

'It's rather a long way—I'm not very sure if I can find it. It's such a long time since I was taken to see him. My Uncle Samuel was always considered a little odd,' he added, by way of explanation.

'Well, odd or not, the sooner we get there, and find out what all this is about, the better.' Scarecrow got up.

'I don't know about you, Mumfie—perhaps the shock has taken away your appetite—but I am feeling distinctly hungry.'

'So am I,' agreed Mumfie. 'I expect when we've had something to eat we will feel better.'

He looked towards the apple trees behind the cottage, which happily had escaped the fire. Some of the apples were rather toasted, but it didn't really matter.

'I always liked them baked, anyway,' said Scarecrow as they walked along through the wood.

Mumfie led the way, looking for familiar landmarks.

'It's very hard,' he said presently, stopping to look about him. 'You see, the last time I came here I was very small, and Papa carried me a good deal of the way. I may even have gone to sleep for some of the journey.'

'Huh! That's helpful. Isn't there somebody about that we could ask?'

'The rabbits might know. They know everybody. Perhaps we could find one of their houses. We will sit down here for a moment and see if one of them comes out. They don't usually appear when people are walking about making noises with their feet, and crackling the branches.'

They sat down under a tree and waited quietly, looking hopefully about them.

'There's one,' whispered Mumfie presently. 'I wonder if it's a rabbit that I know.'

The rabbit, who was half hidden behind a clump of primroses, caught sight of them, and hopped out.

It looked rather hard at Mumfie, and then scuttered across the grass towards them.

'Hullo,' said the rabbit in a nice furry voice, 'how are you, Mumfie? You have been away a long time.'

It looked enquiringly at Scarecrow.

'This is my friend Scarecrow,' said Mumfie proudly. 'Scarecrow, this is Nobkin.'

Scarecrow bowed.

'Do you know anything about this dreadful thing that has happened to our house?' asked Mumfie in an agitated voice.

The rabbit shook its head.

'We heard about the accident, but we don't know how it happened. Strange things have been going on here—but it is best not to talk about them.'

'Well, are we going the right way for Mumfie's Uncle Samuel's?' asked Scarecrow, thinking that the sooner they got to Uncle Samuel, the better.

'Yes,' said Nobkin. 'Keep right on until you come to the rhododendron pool—go round to the boat-house —the forest slopes up steeply behind it, and you'll find steps cut in a path. Your Uncle Samuel's is at the top of the path. Well, good-bye for now—I must hurry— I have some lettuce to attend to.' It hopped away, its white cotton tail bobbing against the dark bushes.

Mumfie and Scarecrow made their way through the wood until they came to the rhododendron pool. They soon found the boat-house, behind which trees climbed up over a steep hill.

'Here we are,' called out Scarecrow who had got a little way ahead. 'Here's the steps. Goodness, but it is a steep climb.' At the top of the steps the trees had been cleared away to form a lane, with bushes planted on either side of it. Half-way down the lane was a white gate. On the gate was a notice—

NO HAWKERS. CIRCULARS. BARREL-ORGANS

OR ANY OTHER RUBBISH

'That is strange,' said Scarecrow. 'I shouldn't have thought there would be any barrel-organs in the forest—or at least not enough to worry anybody.'

'I told you my Uncle Samuel was a little peculiar,' said Mumfie, pushing open the gate.

Inside the gate was a tidy brick-paved path, leading through a carefully tended garden to a pleasant white-washed cottage. In a corner of the garden, Mumfie's Uncle Samuel was to be seen, carefully watering some pot plants through his trunk, which from time to time he dipped in a large green watering-can. The old gentleman was wearing a red checked shirt, tucked

comfortably into a pair of rather shabby blue overalls. On his head, perched between flapping elephantine ears, was a large red flower-pot. Mumfie ran over the grass towards him.

'No Hawkers, no . . .' began Uncle Samuel without looking up.

'Why, bless my soul! It's Mumfie!'

'Uncle Samuel,' cried Mumfie. 'Oh, Uncle, please excuse us arriving so suddenly, but is Mama here by any chance?'

Uncle Samuel looked at him for a moment without replying. He took the flower-pot off his head; carefully dusted it with an enormous silk handerkerchief; put it back again, and drew another deep draught from the watering-can. With careful aim, he sprayed a fine red geranium, which appeared to be planted inside an elegant white panama hat.

Having done this, he picked up the hat; beckoning Mumfie to come closer.

'Nephew,' he said in a deep growly voice, 'I ask you to look at this magnificent geranium.'

Mumfie looked at the plant, and from thence to the flower-pot upon his uncle's head.

'It's a w-onderful fine geranium, Uncle,' he said dutifully. 'But why have you planted it in your panama hat?'

'Perfectly simple,' rumbled the old gentleman. 'The flower-pot was cooler.'

'Oh, I see.' Mumfie sounded rather doubtful. 'But please, Uncle Samuel, is Mama here by any chance?'

'What is today? Go and look at the calendar, boy.'

'It's Tuesday, Uncle.'

'Why, that is peculiar, it has a remarkable similarity to last Friday. In that case, she isn't. No,' he said, as though definitely making up his mind about the matter. 'She is not here any more.'

'Well, please could you tell me where she has gone?'

'I will when you have told me what that Object might be that is standing by my gate. *That* will take some explaining.'

Mumfie glanced round to where Scarecrow was standing, propped against the gate, his hands in his pockets, staring at Uncle Samuel.

'Oh,' said Mumfie. 'I'm so sorry. That's Scarecrow. Come here, Scarecrow.'

'A scarecrow, is it?' said the Uncle. 'Well, it so happens I haven't any. Better tell it to move off. Scarecrows—I never thought of that. I must add a footnote to the notice. Remind me to get some more paint.'

Mumfie was just about to protest when he caught a warning glance from his friend.

'I can see that I shall have to get round the old boy somehow,' thought Scarecrow. '*Peculiar* isn't the word for it!'

'Good morning, sir,' he said aloud, coming up the path. Then he walked calmly over to a pile of flower-pots stacked under a bush, and selecting one carefully, removed his hat and put the pot on his head. It was rather large, and slipped down over one ear.

'Ah!' he said, sighing audibly, and wriggling his shoulders. 'That's better.'

Uncle Samuel, who had been watching these proceedings with considerable attention, came over to Scarecrow, smiling broadly. He wrung him by the hand.

'How do you do, sir—how *do* you do,' he said, pumping it up and down. 'It is a pleasure to know you. So few sensible people in the world that a new one is always welcome. I don't think I can have caught your name correctly. What did you say his name was?' he said in a loud aside.

'Name of Scarecrow,' said Scarecrow. 'But I've retired now,' he added rather grandly.

'Well! Well! It seems odd. I must say I wouldn't have thought it. A young fellow of your good sense and ability should have gone in for something rather more high class. Take me now—I went into the Navy, and just look at me now—just look at me.' He swelled out his chest, and burst into a roar of laughter, as though he had said something tremendously funny.

'Uncle Samuel—the pride of the family. The family's pride and joy—eh, Mumfie? Well what's the use of

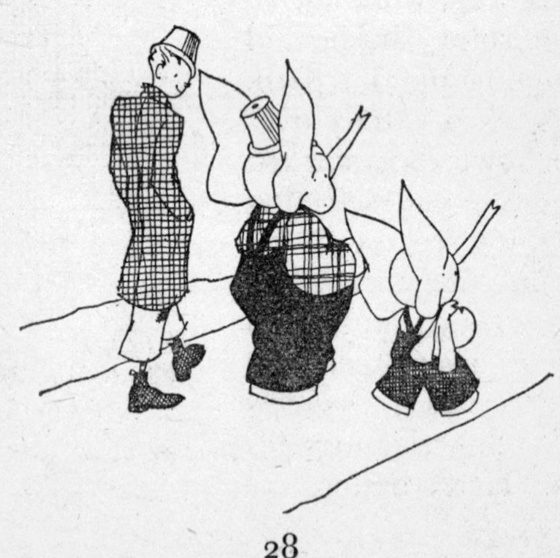

standing here talking, when the sun's well over the yard-arm. Come in and have something.'

'Yes, please,' said Mumfie and Scarecrow eagerly. They trotted beside Uncle Samuel as he led the way into his cottage.

CHAPTER FOUR

'Now,' said Uncle Samuel, who was comfortably settled in a large armchair, a foaming tankard of beer at his elbow. 'I suppose you want to know all about the family?'

'Yes, please.' Mumfie spoke through a large mouthful of home-made saffron cake. Scarecrow, who had just disposed of a bottle of ginger-beer, looked from Mumfie to his uncle, and decided that there was certainly a strong family resemblance.

Uncle Samuel cleared his throat, took the flower-pot off his head, and placed it carefully on the table.

'Hot, isn't it?' he puffed. 'Mumfie, be so good as to go into the kitchen and fetch me a cucumber.'

As Mumfie trotted off, he turned to Scarecrow.

'I didn't want to upset him,' he whispered, leaning forward, 'but you are a friend of his, and seem to have a good head on your shoulders. As a matter of fact, I suspect FOUL PLAY. My sister Belinda was always a careful woman, and I don't believe that house of theirs set fire to itself. Everything gone—lock, stock, and barrel. They arrived here in a dreadful state—no money, you know—honest but poor—can't start re-building without the wherewithal to buy bricks, or wood, or whatever you choose to build with. Always favoured bricks and timber myself. I can't help them much, either, my pension being what it is—ah, thank you, Mumfie. Is that the biggest you could find?'

'Yes, Uncle Samuel,' said Mumfie, watching to see what the old gentleman would do with the cucumber.

He took a clasp knife from his pocket, and carefully cut three pieces, from which he peeled the cool green skin.

He put a strip along his forehead, and handed the other slices to Mumfie and Scarecrow, who followed his example. It was certainly delightfully cool.

'Ah, now that's better,' sighed Uncle Samuel. 'Let me see, where was I?—Oh, yes, Mumfie, I was telling your friend—sensible fellow—I like him. I was about to tell him that your family were here a few days ago. Yes, they came straight to me—nothing like the black sheep when in trouble—you remember that, Mumfie my boy,' he chuckled. 'I put them up for a night or two, while your Ma got over the shock. Told them they could stay as long as they liked—always glad to have them, and your Mama such a good cook. But your Papa was all for going off to the town to look for work. Very sensible idea. I suggested that Belinda should stay here along o' me until he got something—but no, she wouldn't hear of it—nothing for it but that she should go along with him—said if she didn't there would be no one to mend his socks. Mend his socks, indeed! He ought to have been in the Navy.'

He stooped down and pulled off a large gardening shoe.

'Take a look at that.' He stuck out his foot, which was clad in a bright red sock, elegantly darned at the toe. 'There's darning for you. Make and Mend. Every

Saturday. Yes, young fellow, there's nothing like the Navy. I'll bet being a scarecrow didn't teach you to darn like that, eh?'

'Oh, I don't do so bad,' said Scarecrow. 'But you were saying, sir?'

'Oh, yes, where was I? Why, Mumfie, don't look so worried—what a frown—dear, dear, have some more cucumber. You don't need to worry yourself. They'll be all right.'

'Oh, dear, oh, dear!' sighed Mumfie. 'My poor Mama and Papa, they won't like the town a bit. What are we going to *do*, Uncle Samuel?'

'There's only one sensible thing to do that I can see—viz. and to wit—build them another house, and then send for them as soon as it is ready.'

'O-o, yes,' cried Mumfie excitedly. 'That is a lovely idea. When can we begin?'

'Humph!' Uncle Samuel blew rather ponderously through his trunk. 'That is rather the difficulty. If it is to be wood, then we have to buy wood, and if it is to be bricks, then we have to buy bricks, and so the question arises—who is going to pay for them?'

Mumfie fumbled about in his pocket, and brought out three pennies, which he laid carefully upon the table.

'There's something to start with. How much have you got, Scarecrow?'

'Sixpence-halfpenny,' said Scarecrow, adding it to the pile.

'How much have you got, Uncle Samuel?' asked Mumfie hopefully.

'I haven't the faintest idea. Go upstairs and fetch the cash-box, Mumfie—you'll find it in the sea-chest under the window.

'It isn't as simple as all that,' whispered the old gentleman, as soon as his nephew was out of sight. 'Mighty queer things have been going on in this forest. Theirs isn't the only house which has come to grief. Shouldn't be surprised if it were *my* turn soon.'

'Why?' asked Scarecrow, sensing a mystery.

'Well.' Uncle Samuel leant close to him, whispering in his ear. 'There have been LURKINGS in the wood after the sun has gone down. LURKINGS. I've seen them distinctly.'

Scarecrow was just about to ask what a Lurking might be when Mumfie returned with the black cash-box, which he placed on his uncle's knee.

'Go on, sir,' urged Scarecrow. 'You needn't mind Mumfie. He looks very small, but he's up to anything. You wouldn't believe the adventures we've had together. In tight places, it's usually Mumfie who manages to think of something.'

'Is that so.' Uncle Samuel regarded his small nephew with approval. 'In that case that makes things easier. Mumfie, there's been some mighty queer things going on in this forest lately.'

'Yes,' said Scarecrow. 'LURKINGS, Mumfie.' He sat far forward in his chair, feeling excited inside.

'What is a Lurking?' asked Mumfie. 'Hadn't you better see how much you've got in the cash-box, Uncle?'

'Yes, yes. Where is the key? Wherever did I put that key? Have a look in the drawer in the dresser—no, I remember—it's under that primula on the window-sill. That's the way.'

He opened the box, and counted out seventeen shillings and fivepence farthing. He held up the farthing and looked at it in disgust.

'Simply useless. The only people who like them are bakers. Unpleasant, floury sort of people—as far as I am concerned, they can have 'em.'

'They make very nice buttons,' suggested Mumfie. 'How much have we got now? You count up, Scarecrow; you'll do it quicker.'

'Eighteen and twopence three farthings,' announced Scarecrow. 'That should be enough to begin with.'

'It ought,' agreed the uncle, 'if we are not interfered with. But what I am afraid of, is that no sooner do we start building, than the place will get burned down again. That or something else equally useful.'

'But why?' asked Mumfie, puzzled. 'Whoever would want to burn it down on purpose?'

'That,' said Uncle Samuel ponderously, 'is the question. It all began some little time ago, when Badger's house was destroyed in the most extraordinary manner. I saw the ruins myself, and it looked just as though some giant hand had torn it bodily out of the ground. The family were at home at the time, peacefully eating their supper.

'They were all too dazed to give any clear account, but from their broken stories, one gathered that it was as if an earthquake had fallen upon them. At one moment they were sitting at supper, and the next there was a rending, cracking sound, and the whole house seemed to fly up into the air. Of course they all fell out of the windows and doors, even through the floor.

Willie, the youngest, who landed in a bush, and so was not seriously hurt, swears that he saw an enormous pair of legs, quite as thick as tree-trunks, making off through the forest, but it was generally felt that the shock must have over-stimulated his imagination. The industrious Badger pulled himself together and started to build again, and I suppose the incident would gradually have been forgotten, only that was not the end. No, indeed. Soon, several householders, including myself, were approached by unpleasant ferrets, who said that they had called on behalf of a "certain person" whom they refused to name, but who, they said, had authorized them to offer sums of money for the purchase of the owners' houses and property. Of course, people refused to sell. This is a very pleasant forest—quiet and peaceful—nobody who is lucky enough to live here wants to move from it. The ferrets then became extremely unpleasant, and started to threaten. Take the case of your own family. Your Papa got back one evening from his work, to find a nasty-looking little stoat hanging about outside the cottage. Your Ma had tried to send it off, but it had refused to go until the old man returned. Out it comes, as bold as brass, with an offer to buy the house and garden for £20. Your Pa said he had no intention of selling—for twenty pounds, or even a hundred for that matter, and that it was no good arguing about it. He told the creature to be off, whereat it promptly became most offensive. Declared that its master would get the property, anyway, and that it would be wiser to accept the money offered, otherwise he would be liable to find himself without either house, or money. Your Papa, as you can well imagine, sent the creature packing at the toe of his boot; and that was the last he expected to hear of the matter. That was on Thursday. On Friday, as you know, your Mama and Pa make their weekly expedition into Market. When they got back in the evening, the house was burned to the ground. Now I ask you. I put it to you as intelligent people. Does that look like accident? No, it does *not.*'

'It certainly doesn't, agreed Scarecrow.

'And who is this villainous person who goes about destroying other people's houses? What is he doing it for?'

'As to what he's doing it for—nobody knows. They don't even know who he is. If we knew that, we might be able to start doing something about it; but none of his agents will give him away. He must pay them pretty well, for a more untrustworthy, shifty-looking lot, I never did see.'

Mumfie got up, and started to pace up and down the room.

'We must find out somehow,' he said. 'Please could I have some more saffron cake, Uncle Samuel? I believe I have an idea.'

'There he goes,' cried Scarecrow gaily. 'What did I tell you, sir, I knew he would think of something.'

'What you said just now put it into my head,' Mumfie went on, between mouthfuls of cake.

'If only we could capture one of these agents, then maybe we could persuade him to tell us who his master is.'

'If we can capture him, then we'll persuade him all right—won't we, Uncle Samuel!' Scarecrow sounded as though he meant business. 'Do you think one of them is likely to call here again?'

'I wouldn't be surprised. I'm keeping a pretty careful watch, I can assure you. Never leave the house empty. Not running any risks of its being set on fire—I——'

'My goodness!' interrupted Mumfie suddenly. 'Did you hear anyone outside? I thought I heard someone coming up the path.'

Scarecrow went over to the door, just as a note was slipped underneath it. He stooped to pick it up.

'It's a letter for you, sir. Rather funny the postman putting it under the door, when you've got a perfectly good letter-box.'

He suddenly had an idea. He pulled open the front door, and was just in time to see a small dark form sneaking through the white gate. He rushed down the path; but it was away, quick as light, down the steep steps, into the forest. Scarecrow came pattering back into the house.

'No good—lost him,' he puffed. 'Very suspicious-looking character. Couldn't have been up to any honest purpose, scuttling away like that. What's in the note, sir?'

Uncle Samuel slit open the envelope and pulled out a sheet of thick white paper. The letter was type-written. He read out:

Dear Sir,

My agent called upon you on Friday last, with a view to purchasing your house and property, for the generous sum of £50; which offer was, I gather, summarily refused. I enclose herewith a cheque for the above-mentioned amount, together with the warning, that unless you vacate the said property within twenty-four hours, you will be forced to do so by methods which will hold neither profit, nor comfort, to your good self.

The letter was unsigned, and bore no address. The signature on the cheque was so scratchy that it was impossible to make it out.

'Well,' said Scarecrow, taking hold of the cheque, which had slipped on to the table. 'Very obliging of him, I'm sure. Here you are, Mumfie. Contribution Number One to the Building Fund, from our friend, the Enemy.'

He tossed it over to Mumfie, who took it, and looked at it very hard upside down.

'It's a very funny sort of fifty pounds,' he said. 'But I'm sure it will be very helpful.'

'You bet it will! Now, sir—I think we have them where we want them. We'll write an answer to this letter, telling him exactly where he gets off; then we will arrange a nice little reception for his minions when they arrive.'

Uncle Samuel cut himself another slice of cucumber, and placed the peel carefully over the end of his trunk.

'I think you have something there, my boy,' he chuckled.

'A nice reception indeed! Very good that. Brains and Ability. They always count in the end.' He filled up his tankard, and opened two more bottles of ginger-beer.

'To the Enemy!' he bellowed. 'May he be hung by his own bedsocks!'

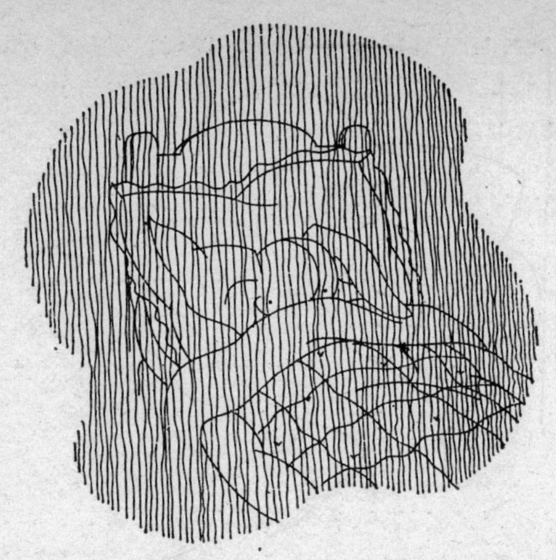

CHAPTER FIVE

Mumfie lay in bed, watching the moon peeping through the half-drawn curtains. Uncle Samuel, after a hearty supper, had sent them off to bed, telling them not to worry, as he would keep a good look-out, and see that no harm came to the cottage while they were asleep. Scarecrow's suggestion that they should take turns in watching, he turned down with some asperity, announcing that he was quite capable of guarding his own mansion, without keeping his guests up half the night. He would brook no argument, and there had been nothing for it but to go off to bed.

Scarecrow, who felt rather tired, was soon fast asleep; but Mumfie lay awake for a long time, thinking about his Mama and Papa, and making up plans for the lovely new house he was going to build them.

The night was very quiet. Occasionally an owl sent its long, wailing hoot through the forest. A breeze blew gently against the curtains. Mumfie was inspecting a

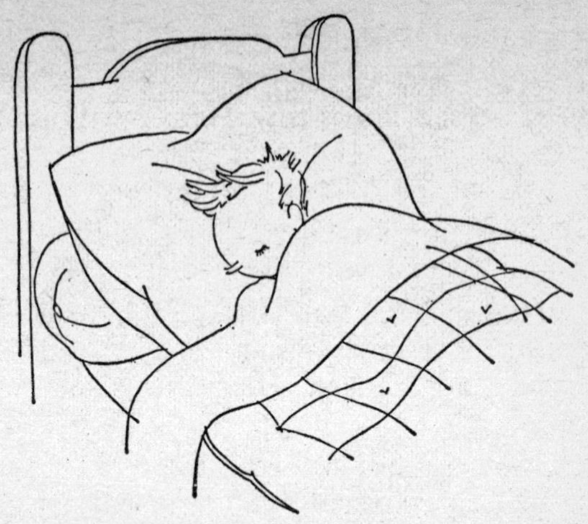

patch of moonlight on his bed, when he thought he heard a stealthy sound coming from somewhere outside the cottage.

He pricked up his ears, and sat up in bed. Yes, there it was again—only a breath of sound, as though something were creeping about outside.

'Scarecrow!' he whispered.

'Snore!' went Scarecrow, and turned over more comfortably in bed.

Mumfie leapt over and pushed him.

'What is it?' muttered Scarecrow. 'What's the time? —Why, Mumfie,' he cried, waking up properly. 'What did you want to do that for—it's the middle of the——'

'Sh!' warned Mumfie, leaning close to him. 'Don't make a noise, Scarecrow; but I'm sure I can hear something moving about outside.'

Scarecrow sat up in bed. Everything was quiet as before.

'I can't hear anything,' he announced rather crossly. 'You must have been dreaming. Anyway, if there is anything Uncle Samuel will take care of it.'

'P'r'aps he's gone to bed. I heard him creaking about

downstairs for some time, but I don't hear him any more.'

'Oh, well,' sighed Scarecrow. He slipped out of bed, and went over to the window.

'The light's still on; I can see it shining on the path. I can't see anything outside. It's such a bright night that I doubt if they would risk an attack. Wait a minute, though. Come over here, Mumfie. Can you see something dark under that bush? There—where the flower-pots are stacked. Humph! I believe you're right, Mumfie.'

'What had we better do?' whispered Mumfie, peeping out fearfully. 'What do you suppose it is, Scarecrow?'

'That? That's a Lurking,' announced Scarecrow with conviction. 'Your uncle said there had been some of them about. We had better go and fetch him.'

They opened the bedroom door, and crept downstairs. Mumfie opened the door of the sitting-room and peeped inside. 'Uncle Samuel!' he whispered urgently.

The lamp was burning, but his uncle was not in the room.

'He's not here,' said Mumfie. 'He must have gone to bed, and forgotten to turn the light off.'

They ran upstairs to the bedroom. They knocked at the door, but hearing no sound, crept inside.

'He seems to be very fast asleep.' Scarecrow went over to the bed. 'Uncle Samuel,' he whispered. 'Here, Mumfie—light the candle. There's something funny here.'

With a trembling hand, Mumfie found the matches and struck a light. The bed was empty, the bedclothes undisturbed.

'Huh!' said Scarecrow. 'Doesn't look as though he's been to bed at all.'

They pattered downstairs again, thinking that

perhaps Mumfie's uncle had gone to the kitchen to get himself a little light refreshment. The kitchen was quiet, and empty. It gradually dawned on them that Uncle Samuel was nowhere in the house.

'My goodness!' said Scarecrow, trying not to sound as alarmed as he felt. 'Here's a nice state of affairs. Hush, Mumfie. Can you still hear anything outside?'

Mumfie listened. 'I don't think so. This is very strange. It's not like Uncle Samuel to go off and leave us all alone; specially when there's a chance of the house getting burnt down.' He went over to the window.

'Oh, my goodness me! Look!' he said suddenly, in a voice that shook. 'Oh, Scarecrow, come and look. Oh, my goodness me!' He ran over to Scarecrow, regardless of the noise he was making, and caught him by the hand. Together they went over to the window, and looked out.

Moonlight flooded the garden, filling with shadow the outline of an enormous footprint.

'Well, blacken my crumpets!' gasped Scarecrow. 'What on earth is that?'

'I d-d-don't know,' stuttered Mumfie. 'It looks very l-l-like a footprint—but it can't be.' He pulled himself together. 'Because nobody has feet as big as that—nobody that I ever saw. Scarecrow, nobody could possibly have such a big foot, could they?'

'No *ordinary* person,' said Scarecrow. 'Come on—we can't really see it properly from here. I'm going out to investigate.'

'But what about the Lurkings?' Mumfie still sounded rather nervous. 'I don't think I should particularly care about bumping into a Lurking, Scarecrow.'

'If it comes to that, neither should I—but I can't help feeling that something must have happened to your Uncle Samuel. It looks to me as if the garden were rather trampled. Come on.'

He opened the front door cautiously. 'I can't see anyone about.' He went outside, followed closely by Mumfie.

On closer inspection there could be no mistaking the footprint, clearly marked in the soft flower-bed which bordered the garden-path.

'The clumsy thing's trodden down all the tulips,' said Mumfie crossly.

'Huh!' Scarecrow scratched his head. 'My feet are pretty large, but just take a look at this.' He put his foot inside the huge outline, and carefully paced along it. 'Twenty-four paces! Someone with feet twenty-four times the size of mine—that's what we've got to look for.'

'Oo-er,' said Mumfie rather commonly, forgetting himself for the moment in his excitement. 'It must be a Giant. Do you really think that we had better look for him, Scarecrow?'

'I'm afraid so.' Scarecrow went over to the window, which was wide open.

'Just look here. See, the paint's all scratched, and some of the wisteria dragged away. It looks just as though something has been pulled through the window.'

'It does,' agreed Mumfie, stretching up to reach something which was caught in a splinter on the window-sill. He held out a piece of blue cloth.

'Scarecrow,' he said in an awestricken voice. 'What colour trousers was Uncle Samuel wearing?'

'Blue,' replied Scarecrow without hesitation. 'I particularly noticed them because they were rather like yours. Here, let me see that. Why, you don't think . . .'

'It looks very like it. Scarecrow, it must have been a very *big* Giant, to be able to pull my Uncle Samuel through the window. Listen—suppose they meant to burn down the house tonight, and the Giant removed Uncle Samuel to get him out of the way, so that his servants could come and burn down the empty house.'

'It's not empty,' said Scarecrow. 'We're here.'

'Yes, but the Giant wouldn't know that. Remember he doesn't know anything about us.'

Scarecrow nodded his head. 'I think you have something there, Mumfie,' he said, in a very good imitation of Uncle Samuel. He caught hold of Mumfie, and dragged him quickly into the house.

'Why, whatever!' gasped Mumfie. 'What's the matter, Scarecrow?'

'Hush!' whispered that hero. 'The Lurkings again. I distinctly heard them, round at the back.' He went over to the fireplace, and seized a poker.

'Grab something, old fellow. This is where we catch them in the very act.'

Mumfie, looking round for some heavy implement, caught sight of Uncle Samuel's stout walking stick, in a stand by the front door. Thus armed, they crept silently towards the back kitchen.

'Hang on a minute,' whispered Scarecrow. He stole over to the kitchen window, and peered through the drawn curtains.

There, by the wall, he could distinguish two shadowy, ferret-like forms, dragging against it a bundle of faggots. On the grass stood a red petrol-tin.

'Humph!' said Scarecrow to himself. 'So you would, would you? Thank goodness the window's open.'

He signed to Mumfie to come close.

'Now,' he whispered, 'wait 'til they are right under the window; then you take the left one, and I'll have the right.'

The two lurkers were now creeping under the window. They were not making much attempt to be silent, thinking, no doubt, that the house was empty.

'That's right,' said one, in an unpleasant, rusty voice.

'That ought to do it. Let's 'ave the petrol, mate.'

He stooped down to push the faggots more securely against the wall, while his mate brought over the petrol-can.

'Now!' said Scarecrow.

He leant right out of the window, and brought down the poker, with neatness and precision, full on the ferret's unsuspecting head. He watched with satisfaction, as it sank to the ground without a cry.

At the same time Mumfie leapt into action. He aimed a terrible blow with the walking stick at the head of the second conspirator. But unhappily, the stool on which he was standing slipped, and he tumbled head first out of the window.

He picked himself up in time to see his quarry scuttering away down the back garden. With a whoop of rage, he gave chase; but it was no use, his stumpy

little legs would not allow him to catch up with the lightning-quick ferret.

'Oh, dear,' he said. 'I'm afraid he's got away, Scarecrow. If only I hadn't fallen out of the window. I was going to catch him such a lovely smack. Oh, but I think he's dropped something.'

He stooped to pick up a small round disk that

glittered in the moonlight. He could make out, engraved on its smooth surface, the number, 153.

'Never mind.' Scarecrow was busy trussing up his victim. 'He's had the fright of his life. I don't expect he will go trying to burn down other people's houses again for quite a while. Come and look at this one—I think it's coming round. Here—help me to drag it into the house. Poof!' he said, wrinkling his nose. 'Dirty creatures these ferrets. Perhaps we'd better take him straight to the coal-cellar.'

'Ow!' groaned the ferret, trying to sit up. 'Ow! My head!'

'Now then,' said Scarecrow sternly. 'Sit up and pull yourself together. You will be required to answer a few questions. Who sent you to burn the house?'

The ferret stared at him insolently through its beady eyes, and said nothing.

'Oh, so you won't talk,' snapped Scarecrow. 'Mumfie, fetch me the poker.'

'Who sent you to burn down the house?' he repeated, waving the weapon in a threatening manner.

'Oh, don't 'it me, mister,' squealed the ferret, rapidly changing its tone.

'That,' said Scarecrow, 'entirely depends on you. Now hurry up and answer the question.'

'I daren't.' The creature looked nervously round. 'If I splits, 'e'll be after me.'

'Well, if you *don't* split, *I'll* be after you; and I'm right here on the spot. You can take your choice.'

'Oh,' said the ferret. 'Looks like I'm in for it either way. Me Mother always said I'd come to no good if I went on the way I'm going. It seems she was right.'

'Don't mumble,' shouted Scarecrow. 'Answer the question.'

'Now you're asking. I can't rightly do that—no, don't 'it me, mister—I'll tell as much as I know. We gets our orders—but we don't know 'oo they comes from.'

'How do you get them?'

'The Fox gives 'em out at the meetings.'

'Whereabouts are the meetings?'

'Oh, go on, mister, I can't tell you that. It's more than me life's worth. Oh, all right,' as Scarecrow brought the poker down within an inch of its nose. 'The meeting-place is in a disused burrow down by the boat-house. You gets in through an 'ole by the boat-house door.'

'When is the next meeting?'

'Meeting to-morrer,' wheezed the creature. 'Ten-thirty. Now let me go, mister.'

'All right. That's about enough, I think. But before you go, I'll have that disk which is hanging round your neck. You won't be needing it any more.'

They untied the terrified ferret, who when released, dashed away into the forest.

Scarecrow looked at the disk.

'Number 31,' he read. 'I expect it's an identification number. What a night.' He stretched, yawning. 'I think we had better go in and get some sleep—we can't do anything much until the meeting tomorrow.'

'But what about Uncle Samuel?' asked Mumfie.

'The only way we will be able to trace him is by what we are able to pick up at the meeting. In the meantime, don't worry, Mumfie—when it comes to Brains,' he said with satisfaction, 'your Uncle Samuel is more than a match for most giants.'

He pushed the sleepy Mumfie up the stairs, and tumbled after him into bed.

CHAPTER SIX

'What's the time?' asked Scarecrow. He was climbing into his coat, having first wound a dark muffler of Uncle Samuel's round his throat. He pulled his hat well down over his eyes.

'Ten o'clock.' Mumfie looked at his watch. 'Do you think we should be starting?'

'Yes. If this meeting is at ten-thirty, we want to give ourselves plenty of time to find the place. Mumfie, it's a pity you haven't got a hat—I'm afraid you don't look a bit like a ferret.'

He glanced round the room. In one corner was a cupboard, where Uncle Samuel hung his coats.

'Here, what about this?'

He took out a rather battered cap. 'Try this. Tuck your ears inside it. There, that's better—specially if you keep your coat-collar turned up. That coat is too big for you, but it is better than your own, specially if you stuff your nose inside it when you get there.'

He had dressed Mumfie up in one of his uncle's old shooting jackets, which covered his own coat, coming right down to the ground. He had turned up the sleeves inside, and the disguise was really very convincing.

'Now let's go. Here, we'd better take that torch.'

He took the key down from its hook, and carefully locked the front door behind them. They looked round to make sure that no one was about, and then went through the garden gate, into the dark, still forest.

The thin sickle moon was hidden behind clouds; it was quite difficult to see their way. Mumfie bumbled down the steep steps, rather hampered by his long coat. He kept close to Scarecrow, for the tall, dim trees made him feel rather lonely. Away in the forest came the soft sound of some stirring animal. The sharp crack of a branch, a rustling in the undergrowth, and then silence, broken only by their footsteps. Suddenly, just overhead, an owl hooted. The long, piercing cry stretched into the silence, making Mumfie jump with fright. He clutched hold of Scarecrow.

'What was that?' he whispered nervously.

'It's only an owl—look, up there in the tree—you can just see its yellow eyes.'

'Of course. How silly—it gave me quite a fright. Good evening, Owl . . .' he was beginning politely, when Scarecrow hissed at him to be quiet.

'Look! Down there by the side of the lake.' He pointed towards the rhododendron bushes, which sprang into shape, caught in the rays of several small, moving lights. 'It would seem that the rest of the meeting is arriving. Come on, Mumfie, the best thing we can do is to mingle with the crowd—then we won't be so easily noticed. There seem to be plenty of them—if we skrit round this side, we will be able to catch up.'

It was evident that the meeting would have a good attendance. Dark, heavily muffled shapes were coming out of the forest, to make their way along the lake; so that when the boat-house was reached, Mumfie and Scarecrow found themselves surrounded by quite a crowd; all dressed very much as themselves, with big coats, and hats pulled down over their eyes.

They were a strangely silent gathering, with none of the chatter that Mumfie would have expected at a meeting. He wished that he were a little taller. It was quite difficult to see where he was going.

He followed the crowd into the boat-house, which one of them had unlocked. He found time to wonder how it had got hold of the key. They filed along past the boat, and the leader pulled back some tackle which was stacked against the wall, to reveal quite a large hole, into which it disappeared. Scarecrow looked round to see if Mumfie were behind him; then into the hole he went. It led into a dark, airless tunnel, smelling of damp earth. After what seemed a long time they emerged into a gloomy chamber, dimly lit by a lamp which hung against the wall. Mumfie looked about him. He could now see that most of his companions were stoats or ferrets, with here and there a weasel. Under the lamp stood a fox, whose yellow eyes held a sly expression as it stared at Mumfie rather thoughtfully.

Mumfie poked Scarecrow.

'The fox is looking rather hard,' he whispered.

The creature continued to stare for a few moments, then it went over to a table at the far side of the room, and sat down. 'Now,' it barked, in a quick, snapping voice. 'Are we all here?'

'I think so,' said an old weasel standing at its elbow.

'Then I will call the roll.'

Scarecrow fingered the identification disk, which he

had hung round his neck, and hoped that it would stand them in good stead. If they were required to answer by name they would be in a pretty plight. But to his great relief, only numbers seemed to be needed. When it came to his turn he called out '31' in a voice which he hoped was sufficiently ferret-like.

'Number 153,' squeaked Mumfie; feeling rather proud of having remembered it without reference to his disk.

'Right,' snapped the fox, when all had answered.

'Now we will get down to business. Numbers 31 and 153 step forward, please.'

Mumfie's heart missed a beat. He peeped at Scarecrow, and seeing that his friend had strode without hesitation up to the desk, promptly followed him.

Scarecrow had been careful to stand with his back to the light. He wished that Mumfie were not quite such a comfortable shape—it was surely very difficult for anyone to mistake him for a weasel.

But the fox was speaking.

'Submit your report on the case of Uncle Samuel. Was the job successful?'

Scarecrow thought rapidly. Should he say that the house was burnt down? The truth would probably not be discovered until morning. Then he suddenly had an idea. It was a risk, but he would take it.

'Everything went off according to instructions,' he wheezed.

'Good,' said the fox. 'Burnt to the ground, I hope?'

'No,' said Scarecrow. 'We received last-minute orders that the house was to be left standing.'

A silence fell over the room.

'Orders from whom?'

Scarecrow thought frantically.

'Direct from headquarters.'

'Let me see them.'

'That is quite impossible.' He took a deep breath. 'I received them verbally.'

'From whom?'

'Naturally I did not see.'

'Then describe the voice.'

'Here goes my last happy moment,' said Scarecrow to himself. 'The voice that rumbles like thunder through the mountains.'

He made it sound as impressive as he could. The words made an immediate and rather startling impression.

The fox, who had been leaning over the table staring at him rather suspiciously, drew back. There was a low sigh round the room, followed by absolute quiet.

Scarecrow seized his advantage.

'Now, Mr. Fox,' he said in a voice of authority. 'I hope you are satisfied with your questioning?'

'Certainly. Certainly. But why doesn't *he* say something?' He pointed to Mumfie.

'Sore throat!' said Mumfie hoarsely.

'Oh, I see.'

'Well, then, I suggest that you proceed with the meeting.'

With great dignity, Scarecrow returned to his place, and sat down. Mumfie followed, trying to walk in an equally dignified manner without tripping over his long coat.

There were various further reports, but from none of them could his friends glean anything as to the whereabouts of Uncle Samuel. Scarecrow was becoming rather bored, when the fox announced that it would read out the orders of the day. After giving various instructions to people scattered about the hall, it called out: 'Number 31.'

'Yes,' said Scarecrow.

'You are to proceed at once to the Forest of a Hundred Pines. Go to the wood-cutter's cottage, where you will receive further instructions.'

'Very well. Will that be all?'

'That is all,' replied the fox. He began to read out the next set of instructions.

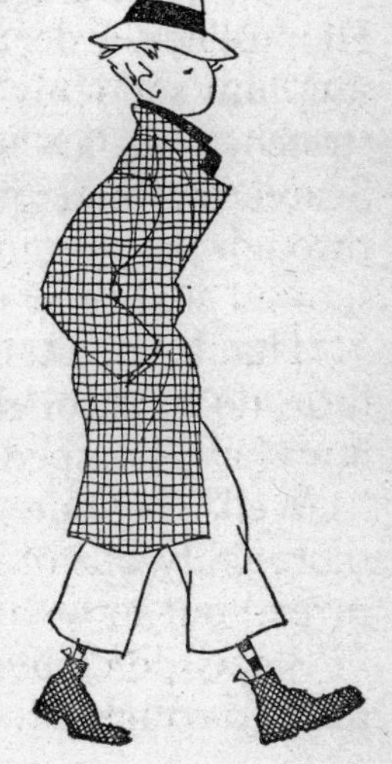

Scarecrow got up and sauntered to the entrance, followed closely by Mumfie, who was feeling so elated at the way they had got through the dangerous meeting, that he forgot to be duly careful about his coat. He was just reaching the tunnel, when his foot caught in the long folds. He stumbled, and, unable to save himself, fell to the ground. Hastily he picked himself up, but alas, his HAT had tumbled off, revealing his large, elephant ears.

There was a bark of rage from the fox.

'Spies!' it shrieked. 'After them!'

'Come on!' shouted Scarecrow, abandoning all attempt at disguise.

They rushed through the narrow tunnel, which served them in good stead, for their pursuers could only follow in single file. Luckily for them, so great was the excitement inside that several weasels became jammed in the narrow opening, and it took some moments to extricate them.

During this time, the friends had cleared the boat-house, and were out in the forest, which was now pitch dark. Mumfie and Scarecrow stumbled about, looking for a place to hide. There were cries from the direction of the boat-house, out of which a scattered bunch was emerging. They could see the flash of many torches, searching about among the thick bushes.

'Oh, my goodness!' gasped Mumfie. 'They'll find us soon if we aren't quick.' He flattened himself against a tree-trunk, as a torch flickered in their direction.

As he pressed against it, he felt the trunk give a little. He pushed harder; and, to his amazement, Scarecrow saw him suddenly disappear inside the tree. Mumfie stretched out an arm, and started to pull him inside. Scarecrow had just managed to squeeze himself through the opening, when a shrilling and scampering showed that their pursuers were on their tracks.

'Thank goodness,' sighed Mumfie, pushing to the little door, through which they must have fallen. 'I must have bumped into a squirrel's house by accident.'

'Well, I hope you're right,' puffed Scarecrow, thoroughly out of breath. 'It would be awkward if it turned out to be a stoat's.'

'Stoats don't live in trees,' said Mumfie. 'I'm sure this is a squirrel's. There are lots of them all over the forest. This must be the back door—the front is always higher up.'

Just then they heard a rustling sound, and a light appeared above them. It bobbed and flickered, casting shadows across a tiny, neat hall, in which they were standing. Someone was evidently coming downstairs.

They looked up, to see a small squirrel in a night-gown; holding a candle before it, and peering down into the hall.

'Why, good gracious me,' cried the squirrel. 'What-ever might you be doing in my house at this time of night?'

'Excuse me, began Mumfie, coming forward, so that the candle-light lit up his round face.

'Why, lawks-a-mussy—if it isn't Mumfie!' exclaimed the squirrel. 'My! How you've grown. Come in and take your things off.' She looked enquiringly at Scare-crow.

'This is Scarecrow.' Mumfie introduced him. 'I'm very sorry to wake you up at this time of night, Mrs. Squirrel, but you see we didn't really mean to. We sort of fell in here by accident.' He began to tell the friendly creature of their adventures.

Mrs. Squirrel listened attentively, her eyes growing rounder and rounder.

'Why, then, you must stay here for the night. You can't possibly go out into the forest again before daytime. It wouldn't be safe.'

She led them upstairs and into her comfortable parlour where she made them take off their things, and warm themselves by the fire, which she stoked up so that it was soon burning merrily. She went to wake her husband, who listened with great interest to their adventures, while his wife busied herself with making some cocoa and preparing a bed for them.

The warm fire, by which he toasted his toes, was making Mumfie feel sleepy. Though he did his best to pay attention to Scarecrow and his host who were busy discussing the best way to discover the whereabouts of Uncle Samuel, his head kept nodding, and he was soon fast asleep

CHAPTER SEVEN

'The Forest of a Hundred Pines,' said Scarecrow, as they tramped along through the wood. 'I suppose you know how to find it, Mumfie?'

'It's a very lonely place.' Mumfie pushed aside a branch from his path. 'People very seldom go there. It borders the mountains that no one has ever climbed. You'll see them presently—we must be nearly at the edge of the wood.'

They came soon to the wood's end, and saw before them a long grassy plain with a solitary road winding across it. In the distance towered blue mountains, with the dark pine forest skirting their misty heights.

'My!' said Scarecrow. 'Have we got to get right over there?'

'I'm afraid so.' Mumfie shaded his eyes with his hand, thinking that it looked a very long way indeed.

'Then I can only hope that this clue isn't a wild-goose chase.' Scarecrow kicked at a stone. 'I'm not really up to all this walking. I'm sure the soles of my shoes are half through already.'

They tramped along the narrow, dusty, hedgeless road. Its surface was stony and uneven.

'Oh, bother!' said Mumfie presently. 'I've got a stone in my shoe.' He sat down by the side of the road to take it out. Scarecrow, glad of the rest, looked back at the wood. It was far behind them, and yet the mountains still appeared a tremendous distance away.

'I don't believe we shall ever get there at this rate,' he sighed. 'I don't suppose many people come along this way.'

He looked at the road, and then suddenly leapt to his feet.

'Look, Mumfie! Just come here and look at this.'

He pointed excitedly to a deep indent in the road, which in this place was rather muddy. Mumfie finished doing up his shoe, and trotted over.

He looked at the print, and then at Scarecrow.

'It looks just like the one in the garden. See if you can find another.'

Scarecrow went on ahead, and presently discovered another huge footprint. 'Yes, here it is,' he sang out.

'Then we are on the right track. By the look of this print the Giant must have come along here quite recently. Do you think that he might live in the mountains? Because if so, then that is where he has probably taken Uncle Samuel.'

'I should think he is almost sure to.' Mumfie bounced along. 'I've always heard that very strange things live in these mountains; and, after all, there isn't anywhere else really big enough for him to live, do you think. Oh, but I do hope we can find Uncle Samuel.'

'We had better get going if we want to arrive there

sometime before next week. It's all very well for a giant—just look how much ground he covers between each step.'

'Hullo! What's that?' He pointed to a dark mass, about a hundred yards ahead, by the side of the road.

'It looks like somebody asleep,' ventured Mumfie.

As they approached, the bundle was discovered to be an old tramp, curled up, fast asleep, his face turned peacefully to the grey sky. Beside him lay a broken-down, rusty-looking bicycle.

Scarecrow poked Mumfie.

'Do you see what *I* see?' he whispered.

'Yes,' said Mumfie. 'It's a tramp.'

'It wasn't the tramp that I was looking at.'

'Oh,' said Mumfie. He looked at Scarecrow, and from Scarecrow to the bicycle.

'It doesn't look as though he is needing it at present.' said Scarecrow casually, rocking on his heels.

'Should we wake him up and ask him?'

Scarecrow looked at the tramp.

'That would seem a pity. Would *you* care to be woken up from a nice sound sleep like that, Mumfie?'

'No.' Mumfie frowned. 'I suppose not. But it does seem a pity. That bicycle would be very useful, Scarecrow.'

Scarecrow went over and picked up the bicycle. The tramp never stirred.

'Yes, it certainly would be a shame to wake him. I think we had better just borrow it.'

'But how shall we return it?'

'That will require a little thought,' said Scarecrow. 'We can think as we go along.'

'Oh, but just think when he wakes up from his nice sleep, and finds his bicycle gone.'

'He probably doesn't need it—tramps are never in a hurry to get anywhere. If he really needed this

Tini

bicycle as much as we do, then he wouldn't have the time to go to sleep.'

Scarecrow mounted the bicycle, and went a little way down the road. Mumfie stood watching him rather undecidedly. He felt a little uncomfortable inside. Then he had an idea. He went over to the tramp and, stooping down, poked him gently.

'Wot!' said the tramp sleepily, brushing his hand away.

He rolled into a more comfortable position, and went to sleep again.

'Mr. Tramp,' said Mumfie firmly, shaking him.

'Wot!' said the tramp, frowning and sitting up.

He stared at Mumfie, and from thence to Scarecrow, who was some way down the road, on the bicycle.

'Hey! Wot's going on here?'

'I'm sorry to disturb you,' said Mumfie. 'But will you be needing that bicycle for an hour or so?'

'Why?' asked the tramp.

'Because if not, we were wondering if you would lend it to us, we're in a dreadful hurry.'

'Why?' said the tramp.

'We are on our way to rescue someone. Every minute is precious.'

'Oh,' said the tramp.

'Then will you?'

'Will I wot?'

'Lend us the bicycle?'

'Wot for?'

'But I've just *told* you what for.' Mumfie was getting a little desperate; he wished that the man could say more than one word at a time.

'I mean, 'ow much?' said the tramp.

'Oh, I see.' Mumfie felt in his pocket; and then remembered that he had put all his money towards the building fund. He called out to Scarecrow.

'Scarecrow, have you any money?'

Scarecrow rode up and dismounted before them.

The tramp stared at him.

Scarecrow felt inside his pockets, and shrugged at Mumfie. He, too, had turned out all his money, which was now locked in Uncle Samuel's cash-box.

The tramp was still staring.

'Natty socks,' he said suddenly.

'I beg your pardon?'

'Socks.' He pointed.

'Oh, those? You like 'em?'

'Yus,' said the tramp. 'Striped. Very natty.' He looked down at his own feet, which were roughly encased in boots and brown paper.

'Huh!' muttered Scarecrow to himself. 'Go on and

pick my socks, *I* don't mind. You don't prefer the muffler?' he asked out aloud.

'Socks,' said the tramp. 'You wants the bike an' I wants the socks. That's fair, ain't it?'

Scarecrow resignedly began to peel them off. His bare feet felt hot and uncomfortable inside his boots, but it was worth it.

'Now,' he asked. 'Can you ride a bicycle, Mumfie?'

'I expect so,' replied Mumfie, who had never tried. 'I've always wanted one. How are we going to get on?'

'I think you had better sit on the carrier, and hold on to my waist. Just a moment.' Scarecrow took off his muffler and wrapped it several times round the carrier to make it more comfortable. Then he held the bicycle, whilst Mumfie scrambled up.

With a good deal of wobbling, he managed to mount, and they started off down the road. Mumfie, peeping over his shoulder, saw the tramp gazing with intense admiration at Scarecrow's socks, which he had managed to pull up as far as his ankles.

'They are very small for him,' he called out.

'Well, it's too late to do anything about that now. He should have thought of that before.'

They sailed gaily along the road. Grey clouds racing overhead seemed to drag the dark mountains nearer.

Scarecrow pedalled with all his might, while Mumfie bounced up and down behind him, singing at the top of his voice.

CHAPTER EIGHT

'Now,' said Scarecrow. 'We must look for the wood-cutter's cottage.'

'Hadn't we better be specially careful?' Mumfie looked around. 'The Fox may have sent some spies to look for us here.'

They had reached the pine forest, which rose above them, dark and mysterious. Scarecrow propped the bicycle against a tree.

'It won't do any harm to keep a careful look-out,' he said cheerfully. 'Though as a matter of fact I should think it is the last place he will look for us after last night.' He peered through the trees, listening carefully, but there did not seem to be anybody about.

'This bicycle won't be much use to us any longer, I'm afraid. I wish there was some undergrowth in which we could hide it. We might need it to get back with.'

'We could lay it flat down, and cover it with bracken,' suggested Mumfie.

They were so busy doing this, that they did not hear someone approaching over the soft pine-needles which covered the earth in a thick carpet.

'There—I don't think anyone would notice it.' Mumfie stood up to admire his handiwork, and saw a child standing a little way off, regarding them.

'Huh!' said Scarecrow. 'That's torn it.'

'Hullo,' he called to the child. She smiled rather shyly, and came a little nearer.

'What are you hiding?' she asked.

'Well, as a matter of fact, it's a bicycle. We thought we could leave it here safely until we got back.'

'Nobody would take it,' said the child. 'Few people come this way. Where are you going?'

'We're looking for a wood-cutter's cottage. Do you know if there is one near here?'

'Why, of course—that is where I live. I'll show you the way. Who do you want to see?'

'We were looking for the wood-cutter. I believe he has a message for us.'

'Oh,' said the child, rather abruptly. Her face clouded over. 'You're one of *them*—I didn't think—you don't look like the others. You can find your own way; follow the path down through the bracken. You can see the chimney smoke there through the trees.'

'Oh, dear,' said Mumfie. 'Won't you come too. What's the matter? You don't look very pleased about something.'

'I don't like you,' answered the child. 'I hate the whole lot of you.' She turned, and began to walk away.

'It is obvious she doesn't like our friend the Giant, or any of his followers.' Scarecrow thought for a moment.

'Don't you think we might safely tell her who we are? She might be able to help us. You catch her up, Mumfie. She will be more likely to listen to you.'

Mumfie ran after the child, calling out to her to stop.

'Wait a minute!' he puffed. It was not easy to run fast over the soft pine-needles.

'Go away,' said the child. 'I don't want to talk to you.'

'But I want to explain,' cried Mumfie. 'Do wait a minute while I catch up.'

He looked so appealing, with his round face and bright, boot-button eyes, that she stopped to wait for him.

'Well, what is it? I don't think anything you say will make the slightest difference—but still.'

'Well, you see, we're not really what you think,' announced Mumfie, breathing rather hard through his trunk. 'We are only pretending to be weasels and ferrets and things. You see, the Giant was burning down our houses, and what's more, he has stolen Uncle Samuel; so we captured two ferrets—at least we almost captured two—but one got away. Then we busted into a meeting—in disguise of course—and managed to hear the two ferrets' instructions—which were to come to this forest and see the wood-cutter. We hoped that we might be able to discover from him some further clue as to Uncle Samuel's whereabouts.' Mumfie took a deep breath.

'Oh, how exciting,' said the child. 'I'm sorry if I was rude. We hate the Giant. He owns this wood—and he's so terribly careless where he treads—he is always crushing down the bracken—only a little while ago he put his foot in our back garden, and ruined all this year's cabbages. We wouldn't do anything for him—only the fox came some weeks ago, and said that if Father didn't act as his agent, terrible things would happen. We might be turned out of the cottage, and not even allowed to live in the forest any more. Father earns his living here, and we have nowhere else to go. He stormed a bit, but gave in in the end—so now the house is often overrun with nasty, smelly stoats and ferrets. They eat everything, and never wipe their boots on the mat. But perhaps you will be able to do something. You and your friend must be terribly brave to go to the meeting like that.'

'Oh, dear,' said Mumfie. 'I hope there are not any stoats about now.'

'No, it's safe enough now,' the child assured him. 'They only come at night.'

Then her face fell.

'Oh, dear, but I'm afraid you will never be able to rescue your uncle. He has probably been taken up to the castle—and even if you managed to get inside, which is doubtful, you would never be able to get out again.'

'We'll see about that,' said Scarecrow. 'The first thing to be done is to get ourselves in. We can think about how to get out again, later. What luck meeting you like this. Perhaps we had better go on to your father's cottage. Do you think he would be willing to help us?'

'I know he would want to—he is always threatening the terrible things he would do to the Giant if he got the chance—but I don't know if he would dare to do very much—there are so many spies. Come along and I'll take you home—at least you can talk it over with him.'

She led the way down through the trees. The young bracken, just bursting into thin, curling tendrils, grew tall on either side of the path. Mumfie thought what fun it would be to play houses in. But, of course, it was no good to think about playing now—they had serious business in hand. He looked at it rather longingly.

'Later on, when I'm not so busy,' he promised himself.

'My, what a nice little cottage. You must be very comfy here.'

'We've always lived here—Mother made the garden. It means a lot of hard work, but she loves it dearly. Come inside. Mother,' she called, 'is Father back yet?'

'Not yet, dear,' said the wood-cutter's wife, appearing from somewhere at the back, where she had been drawing a pail of water.

'Why . . .' She stopped, put the pail down, and dried her hands on her apron.

'I met these two in the forest,' explained the child. 'Come inside, Mum, we've some most exciting things to tell you.'

'Is that dinner?' asked Mumfie rather hopefully. The long bicycle ride had made him feel hungry.

'Why yes, my dears—it's very nearly ready. You are hungry I expect?'

'Well,' said Mumfie. 'Yes, we is—a little,' he added politely, remembering that they had not been invited for lunch, and so there would only be the usual amount prepared. He hoped that the family were not specially hungry. But there was plenty of food for everybody. Mumfie and Scarecrow made an excellent meal, after which they felt a good deal better.

'It's funny what an appetite bicycling gives you,' said Scarecrow, sitting back with a sigh of satisfaction. 'Now I think we had better be on our way. The sooner we get in touch with Uncle Samuel, the better. Could you tell us the best way to get to the castle?'

The wood-cutter's wife looked at them with astonishment. She had listened with the greatest interest to their story, promising to persuade her husband to help them as much as possible, but the suggestion that they should go to the castle themselves evidently amazed her.

'Why, you couldn't possibly go there!' she gasped. 'It would be dreadfully dangerous. What could two little things like you possibly do against a Giant?'

Scarecrow did not exactly care about being referred to as a little thing.

'There's no knowing *what* you can do if you set your mind to it,' he said with dignity. 'Mumfie and I have been in some very tough places before. As far as I can see, no one has even tried to get up to the castle. We shall soon find out how bad it is when we get there. After all, to a Giant I expect I am about as difficult to spot as a grasshopper is to a normal sized person.'

'That is so. I hadn't thought about it in that way,' agreed the good woman. Nevertheless, she continued to look anxious. 'The castle is up in the mountains. It is a very long climb, and a dangerous one too. Without a guide I don't think you would ever be able to find your way—you might become lost in the mists. It gets dreadfully cold up there at night—you would have to try to make the journey by day—but I know of no one to guide you.'

'It all sounds very complicated,' sighed Scarecrow, who to tell the truth was feeling a little reluctant to move after his excellent dinner.

'What do you think about it, Mumfie?'

'Climbing mountains takes a long time, when one's legs is short,' said Mumfie sadly. 'And in the meantime, poor Uncle Samuel is probably shut up in a dismal dungeon—with only bread and water to eat. I wish we could fly, Scarecrow—it's a dreadful disadvantage not being able to fly.'

'Yes,' agreed Scarecrow. 'But we can't—and what is more we have not got an aeroplane—so it looks as though we shall have to walk.'

He got up, thinking that it was a pity they had left their heavy coats with the Squirrel.

'I wonder if you could be so good as to lend us something warm to put on?' He turned to the woodcutter's wife. 'It won't help to get frozen halfway up.'

'Why, of course.' She sent her daughter off to fetch two thick lumber jackets. The child returned with one over each arm.

'My brother's will probably fit you.' She handed a coat to Scarecrow. It was a heavy, checked material. Scarecrow tried it on, and swaggered about the kitchen, fancying himself a good deal.

'You had better have my old one.' She helped Mumfie into the smaller coat. 'I'm afraid it is a bit big for you, but never mind—it will keep you all the warmer.'

Mumfie snuggled into the coat. It was cerainly very warm indeed.

The mother in the meanwhile had cut them some thick bread, which she filled with slices of ham. She did up two packets, which fitted snugly into their pockets.

'There now—at least you will not be hungry. I don't like to let you go off like this—I am sure it isn't wise. But it would seem there is no stopping you.'

'I'm afraid not, ma'am,' said Scarecrow, going to the door. 'Thank you for all your kindness. We will call in again on the way down,' he added cheerfully.

The wood-cutter's wife, and her daughter, after having given them careful directions, watched them as they went away through the tall pines, until they disappeared from sight.

CHAPTER NINE

'Oh, dear, oh, dear!' panted Mumfie in a breathless voice. 'Wait a minute, Scarecrow. I must sit down and puff a bit.'

'Same here!' snorted Scarecrow.

They sat themselves down on a boulder beside the stony mountain path. It seemed hours since they had begun the steep ascent. The pine forest lay straggled below them, tiny now, like a wood on some toy map. It was cold up here; the wind beat chill against them so that they were glad of the protection afforded by their warm jackets. The sky was overcast, with long grey clouds tattered across it, like an old woman's draggled tresses, streaming in the wind.

A wet mist crept stealthily down from the mountain-top, forming delicate, tiny drops on the rough wool of their coats.

'I don't like the look of this mist,' said Scarecrow. 'It's going to be difficult to find our way if it gets any thicker.'

'It seems to be getting worse every minute.' Mumfie looked around him. He felt glad of Scarecrows' company on the lonely mountain-side. The silence was intense; no sound of bird, or tree, or any living thing. The cold grey mountain reared above them to be lost in mist.

'If only I didn't get quite so puffed,' sighed Mumfie. 'I don't feel as though I have any breath at all.'

'That's because we are not acclimatized,' said Scarecrow with authority.

'What is acclimatize?' asked Mumfie, who was sometimes puzzled by the long words Scarecrow used.

'It means that the climate doesn't suit you.' Scarecrow hoped this was right. 'If we lived on this mountain it wouldn't puff us,' he explained.

'Oh, I see. You mean, like polar bears don't feel the cold water because they live in it.' Mumfie shivered. 'There's something to be said for being a polar bear. But we'd better be getting along, Scarecrow—we will never reach the castle at this rate.' He got up and bravely stumped up the narrow twisting path, stopping at times for breath.

The way was not easy; sometimes they had to scramble up rocks too steep for Mumfie to manage alone, so that Scarecrow had to push him from behind.

They had just reached one of these, and Mumfie was balanced rather unsteadily on Scarecrow's shoulders, when they became aware of a darker shadow in the shadows above them.

' 'Elp!' cried Mumfie. 'Whatever is that?' He scrambled up on to the ledge, and peered up into the mist.

The dark shadow descended upon them. Out through the greyness swooped a great bird; the spread of its wings seemed to blot out the sky.

Mumfie gave one loud shriek and started to run across the rock. He felt something grab him by the back of his coat, and he was jerked off his feet and whirled up into the air.

'Ow!' bellowed poor Mumfie. 'Put me down! Oh, Scarecrow! Help! Help!'

He caught a last despairing glimpse of Scarecrow, who was hopping about madly, far below on the mountain path; then the mists obscured him, and he was lost to sight.

Mumfie dared not struggle; to fall now would not help matters at all. 'And not long ago I was wishing I could fly,' he thought ruefully.

He was being carried through the air at such speed that he really did not have very much time to think about anything, which was, perhaps, just as well.

At last they were coming out of the mist. It fell away from them, like a curtain dropped from a stage set in brilliant, stabbing sunshine. Mumfie blinked, and looked around him. The glare hurt his eyes. The great bird flew among the heights of the mountains. Below them banked masses of grey clouds. They rolled softly against the steep rocks like an incoming silent tide.

Somewhere below that thick bank was Scarecrow, alone on the mountain-side.

A tear splashed down on to Mumfie's coat. 'Poor Scarecrow,' he sobbed. But it was hard to go on feeling very miserable in such dazzling sunshine. He stopped crying, and screwing up his eyes against its brilliance, looked about him. There against the mountain-side, whose summit lay bathed in pink radiance, lay a giant castle, buttressed against the rocks. Deep shadows fell between its towers and battlements.

'Oh, *please* put me down!' bellowed the excited little elephant. But the eagle flew on, with Mumfie caught securely in its talons.

It flew right over the castle, so that he could look down upon its battlements and courtyards. Then the bird began to slow its steady flight. It swooped and circled, making Mumfie feel quite giddy. Round in the warm air, planing down until it hovered over a jutting crag, into which was built a large untidy brown nest.

The great bird flew down; and dropped its captive neatly into the centre of the nest.

Mumfie was feeling so giddy that his head swam. He shut his eyes, waiting for the giddiness to wear off. Presently he felt a little better, and cautiously opened one eye. He opened the other, and looked around him.

The eagle had disappeared. Mumfie could just make out a golden speck, lit by the sun. It was quite unbelievably hot. He took off his coat, and then looked with interest around the nest, to where on either side of him sat three baby eaglets, all with their mouths wide open, as if they were expecting some juicy morsel to appear out of the air. They had a helpless air, and Mumfie did not think their gaping expressions particulary becoming. But the eaglets continued to rustle about the nest with their mouths agape. Of Mumfie they took no notice at all.

Mumfie stood up carefully, and undid his collar.

'There,' he said, 'that's better. It's certainly very hot up here. I think I had better get out of here before the eagle comes back.'

He looked around for some means of escaping from the nest. He went to the edge and peered over. Below him was a sheer drop, before the rocks jutted out again, hundreds of feet below. He had a clear view of the castle, shining in the sun.

He looked at the eaglets hopefully.

'Can any of you fly?' he asked politely.

The babies stared at him. They had stopped standing about with their mouths open, and were now huddled rather forlornly in a corner of the nest.

He repeated his question, but no one answered him. They stared at him through round yellow eyes.

'Poof! They aren't going to be any help,' muttered Mumfie. 'Bother!' He sat down rather suddenly. Looking over the steep edge had made him giddy again.

He was gazing at the sky, wondering what he had better do next, when he noticed a dark speck appearing in the distance.

'Oh, lawks!' He got up. 'There's the eagle coming back. Oh, whatever am I to do?'

But though he looked in every direction, there was little chance of escaping from the nest. If only Scarecrow had been there, they might have managed to climb up the steep rocks against which it was built. Scarecrow with his long legs could have managed it. But what was the good of thinking about that. He would probably never see Scarecrow again. He looked again at the eagle, which was now quite close. It circled overhead, the sun gleaming on its wings. Mumfie shaded his eyes with his hand, but could not see very well in the aching glare.

Then he heard a swish of wings. The bird hovered just above him, blotting out the sun. There was a rushing sound, and something dropped down into the nest beside him.

'Thanks for the lift,' said Scarecrow, picking himself up. 'I *don't* think . . . Why, Mumfie!'

'Scarecrow!' roared Mumfie, flinging himself upon him. 'Oh, Scarecrow, I didn't think I'd ever see you again.' He hugged his friend, and then started bouncing about in his excitment, so that it seemed that he might fall out of the nest at any moment.

'Here!' cried Scarecrow. 'Look out or I'll be losing you again. Stand still, Mumfie. All this excitement's bad for my nerves. I can't stand much more.'

'Yes,' agreed Mumfie. 'Yes, perhaps I'd better—but I feels so excited. However did you persuade the eagle to bring you up too?'

'Oh, personality,' said Scarecrow airily. 'No, as a matter of fact I didn't. It had nothing to do with me at all. Very uncomfortable it was too—I was glad that I had that thick coat on—wouldn't have fancied those long talons sticking into my stuffing, I must say.'

'Did it just come and jerk you up, same as me?'

'That's about it. I was making my way up the path, thinking that the best way to find you was to get to the top. I had just paused for a little breath, when something swooped down on top of me and hitched me up into the air.'

'Well, I says to myself—this is one way of getting to the top of a mountain—and it's certainly quicker than I could do it on my own steam. I must admit I felt a little nervous—I didn't relish the thought that the bird might possibly be fancying me as a bit of dinner. Yes, and talking of that, I suppose it's quite likely to be back here at any moment. It has probably gone off to look for the rest of the meal. I think we had better be making tracks—is there any way out of here?'

Mumfie pointed out the rocks above them. 'I was thinking that we might manage to get up there,' he suggested. 'If you were to give me a lift up on your shoulders. Oh, dear, Scarecrow, I do wish that my legs wasn't quite so near the ground.'

'You're all right as you are.' Scarecrow made a back for him. 'That's it. Up you go.' Mumfie climbed safely on to the rock above, and watched Scarecrow following in fine style.

After the first bit the ascent was easier. They came out upon a flat rock by the side of a deep gully.

'Look,' pointed Scarecrow. 'It would be quite easy to get down there. We could practically slide—it's all loose stones. Poof! It's hot. It is a good thing evening is coming on, it may get cooler—and it will be easier to get into the castle.' He tied his coat round his neck, and made Mumfie do the same.

He climbed to the top of the gully, and took a few careful steps over the small, loose scree with which it was filled. 'This is all right—come along, Mumfie,' he called. He took another step, but the stones shot away under his feet, and he found himself tumbling down the narrow ravine, very much faster than his legs could carry him.

'I'm coming!' shouted Mumfie. He started to slide, but could get no foothold. He bounced down the mountain like a rubber ball. They landed in a heap at the bottom.

Scarecrow picked himself up. 'We had better hide among the rocks until it gets dark. It will probably get dark very quickly up here. It's already becoming colder—I should put your jacket on again, Mumfie, it's not much good tied round your neck like that. It wouldn't do to go catching a chill.'

'No,' agreed Mumfie. 'You put yours on as well. Then we could hide behind that boulder, and while we are waiting, it might be a good idea to eat our sandwiches. Mine have got a little squashed—but I expect they will taste all right.'

They crept behind the rock, and sat down under the gathering green dusk to eat their sandwiches.

CHAPTER TEN

'It is dark enough now,' said Scarecrow. 'Poof! and it's cold too.' He pulled the warm jacket closer about him. He looked above him at the stars, sprinkled like gold dust over the sky's dark curtain.

'Isn't it quiet, Mumfie? You can almost hear it.'

They sat still, peering about them, and because they felt rather lonely they moved closer to one another.

'Thank goodness the eagle brought you up too,' said Mumfie. 'I don't know whatever I would have done up here all by myself . . . sh! what was that?'

The silence was broken rudely by a clatter of stones that tumbled down the gully.

'My goodness!' breathed Scarecrow. 'I hope nothing's started a land-slide.' He broke off, and looked at

Mumfie, whose face appeared dimly through the gloom.

'Somebody's coming,' said Mumfie nervously. They flattened themselves against the rock.

Only just in time it appeared.

A strange figure came scrambling and slipping down among the rocks. A funny little man in a green jacket, and a jaunty hat, from which curled a long feather. In one hand he carried a large basket, and in the other a hurricane lantern.

Mumfie and Scarecrow, peeping round the rock, watched him as he set the basket down, and blew out the light in the lamp, which he set carefully against the rock.

He appeared to be counting something in the basket. He shook his head as though dissatisfied with what he saw.

'He might be going to the castle,' whispered Scarecrow. 'Shall we risk it?'

For answer Mumfie nodded his nead, and climbed out from behind the rock.

'Good evening,' he said politely.

The little man looked up in a startled manner. He stared at Mumfie with his mouth wide open.

'Good evening,' said Mumfie again. 'I am sorry if I surprised you, but could you tell us if there is a hut, or some place, where we could find shelter for the night? We have just climbed the mountain, and we feel rather tired.'

'*You* climbed the mountain. Why, I don't believe it. *He* might have, at a pinch, but you, why you're only a baby. I don't believe it's possible.'

' 'Course I climbed it,' cried Mumfie, indignant at being called a baby. 'I did have a little assistance,' he added honestly. 'From an eagle. But I came a good way by myself.'

'But whatever did you do it for? I——'

'To get to the top,' broke in Scarecrow. 'Be a good fellow and tell us where we can spend the night, we've had about enough for one day.'

'You'd better come along with me—I'm just making for home. Climbing mountains for to get to the top. I've never heard of such a thing.' He shook his head.

'Can I help you with the basket?' offered Mumfie, trotting beside the man, as he led the way down a roughly hewn path in the rocks.

'No, that's all right. It isn't heavy. Only eggs.'

Mumfie peeped into the basket, in which lay three enormous eggs.

'My! what big eggs,' he said. 'What are you going to do with them?'

'Give 'em to the cook for his lordship's breakfast.'

'What, all three of them?' Mumfie's heart beat fast with excitement.

'He'll make short work of those. Come on, we will have to hurry.'

Down the mountain they went, until the castle loomed before them, its walls black and shadowy against the luminous darkness of the sky.

Scarecrow and Mumfie looked at each other delightedly as the man went up to a nail-studded oak door, which at his knock was opened from within. Mumfie had time to read a neatly painted notice, which said: 'Tradesmen's Entrance.'

'It doesn't seem a specially big door,' he whispered in a disappointed voice. It would be dreadful, he thought, if the Giant did not live here after all. He dared not ask, for fear of making their guide suspicious.

They followed him down some stairs and along a wide corridor. A delightful smell assailed their nostrils.

'I believe he is going to the kitchen,' whispered

Scarecrow. 'My! doesn't that smell good. I shouldn't be surprised if I were hungry again, Mumfie.'

'No,' replied Mumfie, sniffing. 'Neither should I.'

The man pushed open a door on the right, and went in. Mumfie and Scarecrow followed him, and found themselves in a large, shining kitchen.

Their new friend was talking to a funny little round man with a huge white apron tied round his waist. On his head was a white cap.

'Did you get any eggs?' he asked anxiously.

'Only three, I'm afraid. Here you are—I'll be pushing off now. Oh, by the way, I found these two young fellows on the mountain. They're pretty hungry —you might find them something to eat, and I suppose they can stop here for the night. Climbed the mountain just to get to the top—beats me—but there you are—takes all sorts to make a world—we can't all have our heads screwed on the right way. Well'—he turned to them—'I'll be wishing you good evening. You'll be all right here.'

'I'm sure we shall,' said Mumfie, sniffing the fragrant air. 'Thank you ever so much.' He turned expectantly to the cook, and noticed that a black cat had come in, and was rubbing at his legs, purring loudly.

'Oh, dear, oh, dear!' said the cook. 'Here's Josephine, and her dinner's not ready. So many things at a time, and short-handed too. You'll have to wait, miss.'

'It looks as though we'll have to wait, too,' muttered Scarecrow.

'Good evening,' he said, by way of drawing attention to himself. 'Allow me to introduce myself, Scarecrow.' He bowed. 'And this is Mumfie—but we won't keep you—I can see you are busy.'

He turned and made for the door, beckoning Mumfie to follow him.

'Oh, don't go,' said the cook. 'Come inside and sit down. We are always pleased to have visitors, we see so few new faces up here. We are usually quite straight by this time, but what with one thing and another—the cat's dinner, and the prisoner's dinner—not to mention the master's—my! my!' He mopped his forehead on a corner of his apron.

At the mention of the word prisoner, Mumfie and Scarecrow had glanced quickly at each other.

'You must be dreadfully busy,' said Mumfie. 'You seem to have to cook a very large amount of food at a time.'

He looked towards a huge cauldron, which several cooks were stirring in front of the fire.

'Oh, we do—we do—at it morning and night. You

wouldn't believe how much it takes to feed him. On my feet all day I am—sometimes I wonder how I manage to keep up my strength, indeed I do.'

'But excuse me.' Mumfie looked puzzled. 'Why don't they have giants to do the cooking—it would seem so much easier.'

'So it would, so it would,' agreed the cook. 'But the trouble is that there aren't any. Remarkably short of giants we are in these parts—besides,' he said in a whisper, 'between you and me—giants can't cook. Well, well, there's the soup ready—you must excuse me for a moment.'

He went over to the cauldron, from which several little men were ladling soup into a coloured bowl about the size of a swimming-bath. This, together with knives, forks, and spoons of quite frightening proportions, was placed on a trolley, which was wheeled by the cooks towards a lift.

'There—up she goes,' cried the cook with satisfaction, as the tray disappeared out of sight, propelled by the exertions of twelve little boys.

'There—there's the first course away. Now I had better attend to the cat—please sit down and make yourselves at home—I'll be with you in a moment.'

'Please don't let us disturb you,' said Scarecrow. 'I suppose you will be doing the prisoner's food next?'

'Yes—but that doesn't take long—he's a sensible sized person, like ourselves—catering for giants is quite another story—not that he hasn't a healthy appetite—and glad to see it I am—with the poor thing shut away there, and no one to keep him company. Come to think of it——'

He stooped down, and stared at Mumfie.

'Why, that is really most remarkable—what a likeness! You are not a relation by any chance?'

Mumfie looked fearfully round.

'Sh!' he whispered. 'Oh, dear, Scarecrow, we should have thought of that. I suppose I ought to have put on a disguise.' He wondered whether they dared trust the friendly little cook.

'But what's the matter, you look quite alarmed.' The cook patted him on the back. 'I trust my question didn't upset you? If it did, why, don't answer it—don't answer it. Just forget it.'

'It's very kind of you,' said Mumfie. He decided to take him into their confidence. 'As a matter of fact, he is——'

'Wait a minute,' interrupted Scarecrow. 'We are not quite sure. Would you be kind enough to describe the prisoner.'

'That would not be difficult. Take this young gentleman here, make him a good deal older, bigger, and considerably stouter, you understand, and then you have him. A most remarkable likeness I must say. Don't you agree with me, boys?'

'Yes, indeed,' chorused the cooks. 'A truly remarkable likeness.'

'That's Uncle Samuel all right.' Scarecrow sighed with satisfaction.

'Go ahead, Mumfie.'

'It must be my Uncle Samuel that you have described.' Mumfie beamed. 'Do you know how long they are going to keep him here?'

'I don't, indeed. I can't see the point of the master's keeping him here at all. As a matter of fact, I think he has taken quite a fancy to him. He wouldn't keep him shut up at all, only every time he lets him loose, your uncle tries to escape—very natural I'm sure, and him wanting to get back to his family. But there—I mustn't stop here talking—there is his supper to be got ready, and he'll be clamouring for it.'

'Perhaps—' suggested Mumfie, 'perhaps as you're

short-handed, we could help you by taking it along to him. We haven't anything to do at the moment, have we, Scarecrow?'

'No,' said Scarecrow. 'Nothing at all. We would be glad to be of help.'

'Now I call that friendly.' The cook beamed. 'Did you hear that, boys—the young gentlemen have offered to take along the prisoner's supper—it would be a help, I must say. I suppose it would be all right?'

'Oh, quite all right,' said Scarecrow hastily. 'We're quite used to carrying trays—aren't we, Mumfie? As a matter of fact, I once thought of being a waiter.' He swept up the tray, and flicked a napkin over his arm in a most professional manner.

The cook watched with obvious approval. 'Quite professional, I must say. Oh, dear, oh, dear, here am I

standing gossiping, and I haven't peeled the shrimps yet. Thank you very much. Along the passage, and the third door on the right, then straight down the stairs, and the turnkey will let you in, unless he is off, when he will have left the key on the hook. Thank you—thank you.'

He hurried off towards a basket of prawns, which looked to Mumfie a good deal more like lobsters.

He followed Scarecrow through the doors, whistling gaily to himself, as he thought how surprised Uncle Samuel was going to be, when he saw who it was that had brought him his supper.

CHAPTER ELEVEN

Uncle Samuel sat gloomily in the middle of his cell.

He thought about his comfortable house in the wood which he had built himself with such care and labour. All the years that he had been at sea, he had dreamed of retiring one day to a comfortable country cottage, with a small garden, in which he could grow a few choice flowers and vegetables. Well, at last he had retired, and had found the very place of his dreams. He was extremely attached to the little cottage, where he planned to spend the rest of his days. He sighed heavily, thinking that by this time it had probably been burned to the ground. As to his small nephew, he was grateful to think that he had such a sensible fellow beside him; he would see that Mumfie came to no harm.

'Ah, well,' he said, getting up and stretching himself. 'Once one takes up an adventurous life. there's no telling where it will end. At least it will stop me from getting fusty, I suppose. Heigh-ho! I wish they'd hurry up with my supper. Rum is what I need—a good bottle of rum—I'm getting depressed—I wish I I could see my way to getting out of here.'

He went over to the side of the room, and with great deliberation stood on his head.

'Ha! That's better! When depressed, stand upside-down. The depression will then rush to the feet, where it is no longer of any consequence.'

Uncle Samuel had no sooner delivered himself of this excellent reasoning, when he heard the key turn in the lock. 'Ha! Supper. That's better. That will cheer me up. Come in—come in. . . . Why bless me! bless my soul! Where's me glasses. I can't see so well this way up.'

He stared in amazement at Scarecrow, who had come in, bearing the tray aloft; Mumfie close at his heels.

Mumfie ran over to his uncle.

'Hello, Uncle Samuel,' he said. 'Whatever are you doing standing about upside-down? Isn't it very uncomfortable? Are you surprised to see us?'

'Surprised!' snorted Uncle Samuel, bouncing to his feet with remarkable agility. 'Surprised ain't the word for it.' He rubbed his eyes, and taking a pair of glasses from his pocket, set them firmly on his trunk. 'But, Mumfie, my dear boy, however did you get here—and the admirable Scarecrow too? Don't tell me the Giant made off with you as well?'

'Oh, no, sir,' cried Mumfie and Scarecrow in chorus. 'We found you'd gone, so we set out to rescue you. Have your supper, and we'll tell you all about it.'

They looked rather longingly at the tray.

'Have my supper? Have *our* supper you mean, you both look quite worn out. Plenty for all.'

The friends sighed with relief. Between mouthfuls they told Uncle Samuel of their adventures.

'Now we've got to get you out of here.' frowned Scarecrow. 'It isn't going to be easy, because everything is so big. I've never seen such stairs, we had a terrible job getting down them—nearly bust our legs at each jump. It's going to be a far worse job getting up again.'

'Yes,' said Mumfie. 'Scarecrow jumped, then I handed him the tray, and jumped down myself. It's not so hard for me, 'cos I'm bouncy. What is the Giant like, Uncle Samuel?'

'Hum. That's the funny part. From all the things he is doing down in the wood you would think he was a terrible ruffian. But he isn't—no, not at all—rather the other way—in fact I must admit that he has treated me with a good deal of civility. Almost embarrassing at times. I can't make him out at all—to listen to him, you wouldn't think he would go out of his way to harm anyone. The trouble is he is spoilt—used to having his own way. And then, another thing, I believe he is lonely—there are so few giants about nowadays, that he really hasn't any friends of his own size. Really, if it were not for all the trouble he's causing, I could quite take to him. Between you and me, I don't think he's very bright. A little simple, you might say—he gets an idea into his head, and nothing will get it out again—whether it's sense, or whether it isn't. I took him to task very severely, I can tell you. Burning down people's houses—the very idea! I asked him how he would like it if someone were to come along and burn down his castle. That surprised him. Gave him a nasty jar—said he had never thought of it that way. I asked him what was the idea, if any—but he refused to tell me; put on what I suppose he thought was a knowing expression, but only succeeded in smiling foolishly.'

'Well, if he is so friendly,' aked Mumfie, puzzled, 'why won't he let you go?'

'I told you.' Uncle Samuel wiped his mouth on a check table napkin. 'He's lonely. He has taken a fancy to me—had the impertinence to say he liked the look of me as soon as he saw me through the window. I was playing myself a game of chess at the time; that probably had something to do with it. When he takes a fancy to anything, he just helps himself, and that's all there is to it. What am I to do? If he were anything like my own size I'd soon make short work of his fancies but he ain't—and there you are. He is always muttering to himself about how he wishes he were just an ordinary size—says it's no fun being a giant all by himself on top of a mountain. But that is one of his wishes he *can't* satisfy.'

Uncle Samuel snorted with satisfaction.

'I don't know why he doesn't take reducing tablets.' said Scarecrow. 'Reducing tablets for Giants. That's an idea, Mumfie. There might be quite a lot of money in it.'

'Silly,' said Mumfie, giggling. 'But, Uncle Samuel, if he is really quite a nice giant, I don't see why he went and burned down my mama's house?'

'Just thoughtlessness, I'm afraid. You see he more or less looked upon us as a lot of beetles—and you know, Mumfie, one is not always oneself particulary careful about beetles.'

'Oh, I is,' cried Mumfie indignantly. 'There are lots of beetles who is friends of mine, and I wouldn't think of hurting their little houses.'

'*You* wouldn't, I daresay. But there are a lot of people who do not consider beetles at all. In fact you can pretty well divide people into two classes. Those who consider beetles—and those who don't.' He looked at his watch.

'My goodness me, here we are talking, and it's nearly nine o'clock—they'll be coming for me at any moment.'

'Why?' asked Mumfie. 'Oh, dear, oh, dear.'

'The butler. He nearly always sends for me at this hour to play a game of chess with him. No not the butler, the Giant. Very tiring it is too—you should just see that chess board—about the size of a tennis court—and the chess men—heavy as lead they are—at first it was almost all I could do to lift them—but now he has had 'em put on wheels, so that I can push them about. Even so it's tiring enough. You had better hide somewhere—can't have him catching sight of you, or he will be taking another of his fancies—then none of us will be able to get out. I think you two had better escape while you can—I'll manage to get out of here somehow. Brains against brawn. That's what it will amount to in the end—you see.'

'No,' said Mumfie stoutly. 'We are not going to leave you, Uncle Samuel. We came to rescue you and I am not going to leave until we has. Are you, Scarecrow?'

'Certainly not,' declared Scarecrow. 'But in the meantime I think we had better hide—I can hear someone coming down the passage. Go on eating as though nothing has happened, sir—we'll hide behind the table.'

They just managed to slip behind the heavy cloth in time. They peeped round as an attendant came into the room. He carried two long sticks, with wedges on either side of them.

'Now, sir,' he said to Uncle Samuel in a brisk voice. 'Time for the evening game, if you would be so good. I trust you found your supper to your liking?'

'Oh, very good, very good.' Uncle Samuel laid down his fork. He took one of the sticks from the butler.

'I wonder what that's for?' whispered Mumfie.

'Sh!' Scarecrow caught hold of him.

They watched attentively, while Uncle Samuel

climbed on to the wedges on either side of the stick, and started to bounce up and down high into the air.

'Well, I never!' giggled Scarecrow, as the old gentleman and the butler bounced out of the room, hoppety-hop. 'So that's how they get about. I wondered how they all managed. It must be quite difficult to do it up the stairs though. Come on, I think it's safe to come out now. Thank goodness Uncle Samuel remembered to leave the door open. If only we could find some of those sticks, Mumfie, it would be easy to get about. We had better get out of here before someone comes for the tray.'

They crept through the door, and into the passage.

'Didn't Uncle Samuel look funny?' spluttered Mumfie, as they went along. 'I wonder where they keep those sticks?'

'On the ground floor, I hope,' said Scarecrow. 'Otherwise, we're done.'

'I don't know how we are going to climb these stairs, Mumfie—one thing—there's only five of them. Look, I can only just reach over the top.'

Scarecrow put his hands on the ledge and managed to haul himself up. He dragged Mumfie after him. When they reached the top they were both quite breathless from their exertions. They went along the passage, and past the kitchens.

A door on the left opened suddenly, and a little man in a green baize apron scuttled out. He carried a long saw under his arm.

'I wonder what he is doing?' whispered Scarecrow.

They watched the little man out of sight, and then quietly peeped through the door, which he had left open. Inside was a tremendous noise of sawing and planing. The place smelt pleasantly of wood and resin. A great many little men were busy making chairs and other pieces of furniture, of such giant proportions that they were obliged to use scaffolding and ladders. The floor was thick with shavings. On pegs, just inside the door, were hung rows of green aprons.

'Come on,' said Scarecrow. 'This is where we take to carpentry.'

He went boldly into the room, and took an apron off its peg. He handed one to Mumfie.

'Now roll up your sleeves, and look as businesslike as possible,' he whispered.

'But what are you going to do?' Mumfie looked rather nervously at the double saws that were being drawn to and fro through a log of wood near the entrance.

'The sticks. They are probably made in here.'

Scarecrow walked carelessly across the room, looking for a likely cupboard. To Mumfie's relief, no one appeared to take the slightest notice of them. He poked Scarecrow joyfully as his eye lighted upon a cupboard lined with tall round sticks.

Scarecrow calmly searched about among the racks.

Here's a little one which you ought to be able to manage. I'll take this one.'

They hurried to the door, hung up the green aprons, and ran outside, closing it behind them.

Mumfie climbed on to his stick, and started to bounce up and down. It was not easy at first, and he fell off several times. The stick, which was new, bounced him high into the air.

'Oh, Scarecrow, this is fun!' he cried, hopping about.

Scarecrow, with an air of great concentration, was leaping up and down the passage.

'The harder you bounce, the higher you go,' he called out. 'Now we'd better try for the stairs. I want to have a look round this place. But for goodness' sake don't fall off, Mumfie.'

'I'm a kangaroo,' sang Mumfie happily, as he shot along the passage.

CHAPTER TWELVE

The stairs were not at first easy; Mumfie fell down several times, and Scarecrow did not fare much better.

'Well,' he said, when at last they were able to keep their balance well enough to hop from step to step, 'that's that. But this isn't getting us any nearer to rescuing Uncle Samuel. I wonder what time the Giant goes to bed?'

'He will probably stay up a terrible long time if he is playing chess,' guessed Mumfie, who was beginning to feel a bit sleepy. He yawned. 'I'm feeling sleepy, Scarecrow. Are you? I think my brains would work a bit better if I were to have a little nap.'

'I must admit I've had about enough for one day.' Scarecrow stretched. 'Maybe if we could find a place to sleep, we should think of something better in the morning. At the moment my head is perfectly blank. I wonder where the bedrooms are? Up here, I should think.'

He hopped up some further stairs, and came out upon a landing, at the end of which was a large white-painted door. 'Let's have a look in here. There doesn't seem to be anyone about.'

By bouncing upon his stick he managed to turn the handle. They stole inside.

'What an enormous bedroom,' said Mumfie. 'And *what* an enormous bed. Oh, my goodness—do you suppose this is the Giant's bedroom? We had better go, Scarecrow.'

'No, wait a minute.' Scarecrow frowned thoughtfully. 'If this is the Giant's room, I think I have an idea. Oh, dear I wish I wasn't so sleepy. I can hardly collect my thoughts.'

'It's very hard to collect one's thoughts when one is sleepy,' agreed Mumfie. He walked about the room 'Scarecrow, it would be quite difficult for the Giant to do anything very much if he was dreadfully sleepy, wouldn't it?'

'I expect so. But we don't know if he is a sound sleeper.'

'Maybe we could mix him something to make him sleep well,' suggested Mumfie. 'You know—a sort of nightcap.'

'That's not a bad idea. What should we put in it?'

'Have you any idea what goes in a sleeping-draught, Scarecrow. Look, there's a big glass by his bed, so he must be used to taking something at night.'

He bounced up on to the bed, so that he could sniff the contents of the glass.

'This seems to be lemonade. I don't think lemonade is a very good idea. I think we should find something to add to it. Look in that cupboard over there, Scarecrow. It seems to be some sort of medicine chest.'

Scarecrow climbed up on a table, and opened the cupboard, which was filled with a great array of jars

REDUCING TABLETS

and bottles. He began to read out the labels, while Mumfie listened at the door, to make sure there was nobody coming.

'Cinnamon. Cough Cure. Syrup of Figs. Purple Pills for Pale Giants,' read Scarecrow. 'I don't think any of those would do. Wait a minute—what's this?'

He looked at two large bottles which stood side by side on the lower shelf.

One was marked—

REDUCING TABLETS
Very Strong

The other—

DOCTOR NOD'S SLEEPING MIXTURE
Guaranteed without Snores

'Here's the very thing!' he cried delightedly. He reached out his hand for the bottle.

At that moment there was a noise outside.

'Oh, help!' squealed Mumfie. 'There's somebody coming. Quick, Scarecrow!'

Scarecrow snatched the bottle, and hopping over to the bedside, quickly poured the contents into the glass of lemonade.

The door began slowly to open.

The friends had just time to turn out the light, and scamper beneath the big bed, when the light was switched on again, and they watched from their point of vantage two gigantic feet come into the room.

Scarecrow looked at Mumfie and Mumfie looked at Scarecrow. They flattened themselves down against the carpet, making no sound. There was an alarmingly loud creaking, as the Giant sat down on his bed, and started putting on his slippers. He yawned, and the

sound was like a thunderstorm approaching over the hills. They could hear him pottering about. When he brushed his teeth it reminded Mumfie of nothing so much as his mama sweeping out the yard with a stiff broom. In between scrubs, he sang to himself, which was fortunate, because at that moment Scarecrow took a deep breath of dust, which caused him to sneeze.

'Sh!' cautioned Mumfie, horrified.

'It's all right,' whispered Scarecrow. 'He can't hear with that noise going on. When he hums it's like a full choir. Goodness knows what it would be like if he sang at the top of his voice.'

'Tra! La! La!' sang the Giant. 'Tra-la-la-i-diddle-dee!

'Rat-a-pom!—I've got a little elephant.

'Tra-la-pom! I won the chess, I did. I'm clever, I am. Tra-la-pomm-pomm! Oh, well—bedtime. OH! AH!' He yawned again.

Mumfie put his hands over his ears. Above him a loud creaking announced that the Giant had climbed into bed.

'Now for my nightcap,' he said. 'Oh, where's my book? Where have they put my book? What was I reading? Oh, dear, oh, dear, nobody looks after me—nobody pays any attention to me. Oh, *dear*, oh, dear. Where's my hot-water bottle? Oh, there it is—they will put it too low down—they *know* I like to sit on the hot part.' He fumbled about, and must have found the book, for they heard him turning the pages.

'Where was I? *The Adventures of Tom Thumb*, page fifty-three. That's it.' A contented sigh.

'Don't say he is going to forget the sleeping-draught,' whispered Mumfie in a frightened voice.

They waited patiently, but with growing despair, as the Giant turned over page after page of his book.

Mumfie, from sheer tiredness, was just dropping off to sleep when he was roused by a sound just like the bath-water running out.

'There he goes,' chuckled Scarecrow.' Here, you mustn't go to sleep, old thing—as soon as he is safely off, we shall have to be up and doing.'

Presently the pages ceased to turn, and after a little while the room was shaken by heavy snores.

'That's funny,' said Scarecrow. 'The bottle said the stuff was guaranteed snoreless.'

The Giant continued to snore, but the rumblings gradually became softer, so that they ceased to sound like a great many hippopotami enjoying themselves in a stream, but were mere ordinary snores; the sort of thing in fact that you might expect from Uncle Samuel.

'It must be working now,' pronounced Scarecrow. 'They are getting less and less. I should think we would be safe to come out. Here, wake up, Mumfie.' He poked the sleeping Mumfie, who was lying, his head pillowed on his arms.

'Oh, what!' Mumfie sat up. 'Is it time to get up already? My! the bed's hard. What's happened—where am I?'

Then he remembered that he was not safely tucked up at home, but underneath the bed in the Giant's bedroom.

'Oh, dear—is he asleep, Scarecrow?'

'Yes—fast asleep. We can come out now.'

They crept out from under the bed, and jumped up on to a chair, on which the Giant's clothes were flung in an untidy pile. From here they could see the occupant of the huge bed. They stared at the bed in amazement.

'Why, where's he gone, what has happened?'

Scarecrow looked from the figure asleep in the bed,

to the tumbler, lying empty by the bedside. He picked up the bottle, which in his haste he had dropped, so that it slithered away across the floor. By the flickering firelight he made out the label—

REDUCING TABLETS
Very Strong

'Mumfie!' he gasped. 'I've given him the wrong medicine.'

The medicine had evidently worked, for inside the bed, lost in its vast sheets, lay a head certainly no bigger than that of the average man. Of the Giant there was no sign at all.

'Huh!' said Scarecrow. 'Maybe I didn't do so badly after all. Better look out though—he may wake, up at any moment.'

'I think,' said Mumfie, frowning rather solemnly, 'that it would be quite a good thing if he did, Scarecrow.'

'Oh, do you?' Scarecrow was not certain of this. 'Why?'

'Because now he is not so much bigger than us it might be a good plan if we gave him a talking to. After all, he has no business to go burning down people's houses, even if he does only think about them as beetles. Yes—I think I shall wake him up while he is still small. After all, we don't know how long that medicine is going to work for. I wouldn't be surprised if he were to start getting bigger again quite soon.'

With an air of determination, he scrambled up on to the bed, pulling himself up by the quilt.

Scarecrow shrugged, watching the proceedings from his perch on the chair.

'You will have these ideas, I know.'

Mumfie walked over the bed towards the red head.

He took a curl between his finger and thumb, and gently pulled it.

'Wake up,' said Mumfie.

'He's a terrible sound sleeper.'

He was just going to pull again, when the little giant groaned, and turned over, upsetting Mumfie, so that he fell on to the soft pillow.

'Wake up!' said Mumfie again. 'We want to talk to you, while you're still a reasonable size.'

'What,' mumbled the Giant. 'Before I get what? Eh! Oh! What do you want? What did you want to wake me for—I was just dreaming a nice dream about Tom Thumb? Here—who are you? What's going on here? Where am I? What's happened to the bed?'

He sat up. He looked round the room. Then he rubbed his eyes, and pinched himself.

'But I must be dreaming. I *know* I should never have eaten those shrimps.'

He looked round the room in evident astonishment.

'Why, the room's got bigger—it can't have—there must be something wrong with my eyesight—I shall have to see about getting some glasses.'

He turned his head, shaking it in a bewildered manner—and saw Mumfie looking up at him.

'Why, Uncle Samuel! Whatever are you doing here at this time of night? You've grown—why bless my soul how you've grown. You must be almost as big as me. That is splendid—however did you manage it? Now we shall be able to have the wheels taken off the chessmen. Ha! Ha! This is excellent—I always thought you were highly gifted.'

'Oh, do stop talking so much,' interrupted Mumfie. 'I'm not Uncle Samuel, and I haven't grown. It is you that have shrunk.'

'What do you mean, I have shrunk?' The Giant looked so dreadfully puzzled that Mumfie felt quite sorry for him.

'Why, no—you're not Uncle Samuel—I can see that. You are much younger—quite a child, in fact—you're remarkably like him, though—oh, dear, oh, dear—shrunk, you said?'

'Yes, shrunk,' said Scarecrow from the chair. 'And if you don't believe it, hop out of bed and take a look at yourself in the mirror. Only take care how you get out of bed, or you'll probably fall and hurt yourself.'

The poor giant rubbed his head again, and began to scramble out of bed.

'I suppose you are right,' he muttered. 'I don't feel well. I feel as if something terrible has happened.'

He got as far as the edge of the bed, and looked over. 'What a drop! I think I had better take your word for it.'

He pushed himself back into the middle of the bed again, and looked from Mumfie to Scarecrow, rather helplessly.

'Now,' said Mumfie, taking a deep breath, 'I'm afraid I shall have to speak to you very severely. What

I want to know is—why have you been burning down other people's houses?'

'Oh, that,' said the Giant. 'My, but you *are* like Uncle Samuel. He was only saying the other day——'

'Stick to the point, please,' said Scarecrow.

'But I'm tired of that question. I was telling Uncle Samuel, I never thought about it in the way he did. It all happened so simply—I was just walking about one night, taking an evening stroll, when I came to that little wood. It occurred to me then how much pleasanter it would be to live down there, than up here on the mountain where I never see anyone but the mountain goblins who work for me, and such people as I have been able to bring here. It's dreadfully lonely being a giant, you know—when you are the *only* giant.'

'Stop being sorry for yourself, and get on with the explanation,' ordered Scarecrow severely. He sat down comfortably on the pile of clothes.

'It seemed such a nice wood—and I thought I might clear away some trees and build myself a country cottage there. Somewhere to go in the week-ends—you know the sort of thing. I made a closer inspection, and found a lot of little doll's houses planted here and there. I pulled one right up out of the ground, and was surprised when a lot of little beetles and things fell out.'

'Beetles and things,' cried Mumfie indignantly. 'Why, they were people, just like you and me. How would you like it if someone much bigger than you were to come along and pick up this castle and tip you out, as if you were of no account at all?' Mumfie positively swelled with indignation.

'There you go—talking just like Uncle Samuel again. Don't get sore at me—I tell you, it never occurred to me that way. The burning wasn't even my idea. It did rather puzzle me as to how I was going to get the rest of the doll's houses out of the way, so I pulled up a few trees, and sat down to think it out. I wasn't very full of ideas—in fact I think I was just dozing off to sleep, when I felt something tickle my face, and saw a small red fox sitting just under my chin. I was going to brush it off, when it started to bark, and I could see it was trying to say something to me. Well, we got into conversation—I have so few people to talk to you know—and I do care for conversation. The end of the matter was that I explained just what I had been thinking about the little house I would like to build. The fox clearly saw my difficulties—a very clever fellow he was—simply full of ideas. He said that if I would leave the whole matter to him, for a small remuneration he would be glad to arrange it for me—said he had lots of friends in the forest who would be ready to help for a small fee. Of course I have so much gold I simply don't know what to do with it—just get the gnomes to dig it out of the mountains whenever I want it—so that part was easy. We arranged the price, and I told him to get on with it. That's really all there is to it.'

'Oh, no, it isn't, said Mumfie. 'You might as well know that your horrid fox friend burned down my mama's house, and now she hasn't anywhere to live—she and papa had to go off into town to get work.' Mumfie was near to tears at the sad thought.

'Oh, dear, oh, dear!' sighed the Giant. 'How very sad. What a lot of trouble I've caused—and I only wanted to build myself a country cottage. Oh, dear, dear, dear. Where is my handkerchief?—I feel quite upset.'

He sniffed audibly, and fumbled about under the pillow.

'There it is,' said Mumfie. 'Just beside you.'

'Oh, thank you, thank you. Why, this isn't my

hankie—this is a sheet. Whatever has happened to the bedclothes? Oh, but of course, I forgot—I'm not a giant any more.'

He blew his nose on a corner of the vast handkerchief, and looked at Mumfie tearfully.

'I haven't finished yet,' announced Mumfie. 'There's another thing. It's all very well you enjoying yourself playing chess with Uncle Samuel every evening—but have you thought what *he* feels about it?—you very nearly had his house burnt down too, you know—we were only just in time to stop it. How do you suppose Uncle Samuel likes being shut up here with nobody but you to talk to?'

'But he *likes* playing chess with me,' wailed the Giant. 'He plays a very fine game. You aren't going to take him away, are you? I haven't been so happy for years. I can't spare him—really I can't.' He burst into loud sobs, which were muffled in the handkerchief.

'You are a very selfish giant,' said Mumfie sternly. 'You never think of anyone but yourself. It's probably not altogether your fault,' he added, more kindly. 'It must be hard to be the only giant about—still it doesn't look as though you will have to bother about that any more—you really are not a giant at all now. You can thank Scarecrow for that. He gave you the reducing medicine,' he added proudly.

'Why, no—I suppose I'm not. I'm not a giant—I'm not a giant.' The Giant frowned, letting the idea sink in. 'Why, jumping beans!' He got up. 'Then I needn't go on living here all by myself—I could come down into the wood, and take quite a small house—and I could come quite often to Uncle Samuel's home, and play chess with him. Hurrah! Hurrah!'

He started to dance about the bed, waving his arms with excitement.

Mumfie, who was always pleased to see anyone happy, began to dance round after him. He almost forgot that he was speaking to the Giant very severely.

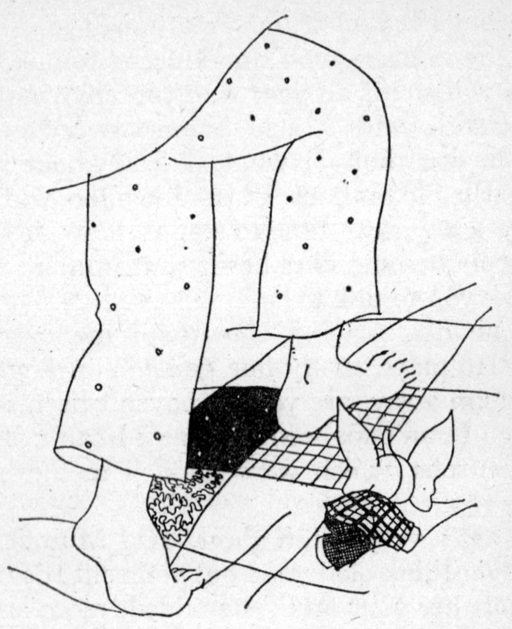

'He could do that, couldn't he, Scarecrow?' he said. 'And he's got lots of money, so he could help us to build a new house for mama and papa—then we'll all be happy.'

But Scarecrow did not seem to be paying attention. He was watching the Giant, who was still capering about the bed.

'Mumfie!' he called sharply, 'I believe he is growing again.'

Sure enough, under their eyes, the dancing Giant became rapidly bigger and bigger.

Mumfie hastily scrambled to the side of the bed to get out of his way.

'Oh, do stop bouncing,' he cried. 'You'll have me off.'

The Giant gave a few more skips, and then suddenly stopped.

'Oh, what's happened?' he wailed. 'Why, the room is getting smaller again. No, I'm getting bigger—oh, stop me, somebody! Where's the bottle—what have you done with the bottle?'

Mumfie clung to the edge of the bed.

'Here it is.' Scarecrow waved it. 'But I'm afraid it isn't any good—you see I gave you the whole lot. That's probably why it worked so well.'

The Giant sat down on the bed and started to sob loudly. Mumfie and Scarecrow covered their ears with their hands. Great tears splashed like waterfalls upon the quilt.

'Never mind,' shouted Mumfie. 'You can get some more. If you go on taking it all the time, you'll probably stay small. Where did you get it? You can easily send for some more.'

'But that's just it,' sobbed the Giant. 'I can't. There only was the one bottle. I bought it from a pedlar—you know—one of those people who come round to the back door. I really wouldn't have bought it, only it is so nice having somebody to talk to. I don't know where he's gone—I should never be able to find him again.'

Mumfie looked at Scarecrow.

'That does make it awkward,' he said. 'What did the pedlar look like?'

'Oh, just a tramp. He came round to the door on a bicycle.'

'On a bicycle?' said Mumfie and Scarecrow together. 'Natty Socks! I wonder if it could be.'

'What's that?' snuffed the Giant. 'You don't know him, do you?'

'I don't know,' said Scarecrow. 'It's only a chance, but we might. Look, I tell you what we will do. If it's the person we think, then probably he won't have got very far, because as a matter of fact he sold us his bicycle. We will take Uncle Samuel home right away, and at the same time we will see if we can find him. If we do, we will send you up some of the bottles at once. In fact we had better give him a standing order for them. We could send them up by pigeon.'

'Dear me—you are kind.' The Giant dried his eyes. 'I really don't deserve it. I shall have to make it up to you somehow. I know what I will do. I will build your family a beautiful palace in the wood. That's what I'll do. You can start right away—order any materials you fancy—hire the workmen at once. Get everything you want—spare no expense—gold—silver—marble—parquet—anything. An enchanting idea.' His face cleared, and he beamed at them.

'Thank you very much,' said Mumfie. 'But they would not care for a palace—they would much rather have a nice little cottage, just big enough to be cosy in—like we had before—only my room a bit bigger, to make room for Scarecrow.'

'Oh, dear.' A huge sigh shook the bed. 'That is a pity. I should have enjoyed building a palace. But never mind—I must not think of myself—build what you like.'

'Then that's settled.' Scarecrow yawned. 'It must be nearly morning. I think we had better start after breakfast, Mumfie. The tramp won't travel very far in the night, I don't suppose, and anyway he won't find walking very comfortable in those socks of mine. I think we had all better go to sleep—then we can start comfortably after breakfast.' They climbed into bed. one on either side of the Giant, and were soon fast asleep.

CHAPTER THIRTEEN

'Carefully, Uncle Samuel,' warned Mumfie, as his uncle slithered down the mountain-side. 'We can't have anybody breaking their legs, you know.'

'No, indeed,' agreed Uncle Samuel, stopping to mop his face. 'Dear me, I'm not at all sure that it isn't more tiring getting *down* a mountain, than it is going up.'

'Quite a lot of people have found that,' agreed Scarecrow. 'It's so dreadfully jarring to the legs—I'm sure my stuffing's coming all unput. Never mind—I don't think it's far now, and once we reach the wood you can have a rest at the wood-cutter's cottage. We can return the coats at the same time.'

'Perhaps it would be a good plan if we left Uncle Samuel at the cottage,' suggested Mumfie. 'I don't see how we are all three going to get on the bicycle. We could come back for him as soon as we have found Natty Socks.'

'That is a good idea.' Uncle Samuel really did look quite done up. 'I will rest a little, and then come along quietly. Maybe if I am lucky I shall get a lift; hitch-hiking I believe it is called—why hitch, I can't fathom, and hike is frankly vulgar—but still, if it gets me a lift I suppose I shouldn't grumble.'

After about half an hour's travelling, the friends left Uncle Samuel comfortably settled before the fire in the woodman's cottage. They said good-bye, and went off to find the bicycle.

The thick bracken had kept the machine nice and dry. Scarecrow wheeled it out of the wood, and they clambered on.

'Won't we be able to build a lovely house!' shouted Mumfie, as they sped along the white, dusty road. 'I don't think the Giant is a bad giant really—he will probably be much better if we can make him an ordinary size.'

'I think half his trouble is being so much by himself.' Scarecrow wobbled over a bump. 'Oo-er! We nearly came off then. This must be about where we found Natty. Look—he has left a paper-bag and a bottle behind.'

'Tramps is so untidy,' said Mumfie, 'cluttering up the countryside. I wonder how far he has gone?'

They bicycled on until they reached the fringes of Mumfie's forest.

'The bicycle isn't going to be much good to us here,' said Scarecrow reluctantly. 'I suppose we had better leave it. We can come over for it later.'

He climbed off, and helped Mumfie down.

'Poof! me legs is stiff,' announced Mumfie, bending up and down.

'They'd be stiffer still if you'd been doing all the pedalling. Ah, well! However are we going to find Natty in here?'

He looked up among the tall trees. The sun filtered greenly through the leaves. It felt cool, and the shade was pleasant after the glaring, dusty road.

'Don't tramps make signs on house-gates?' said Mumfie. 'To show other tramps if the occupants is friendly, and good for a meal or not?'

'Why, I believe they do. Where is the nearest house, Mumfie? He would probably have tried there for breakfast.'

Mumfie paused to think.

'There's a tree-house where some monkeys live not very far away. We might try there.'

They went on to the monkeys' house, and sure enough, on the front door, they found a crudely chalked circle.

'That means he has been lucky,' pronounced Scarecrow, who was not really sure, but very much hoped that this would be the case. 'In that case, he is probably not far away, having his breakfast.'

Mumfie sniffed the air through his trunk.

'I think I smells smoke. Yes, look over there.' Away through the trees they saw a wisp of smoke curling up through the branches.

'Hurrah! shouted Mumfie and Scarecrow together. 'That'll be him. Come on.'

As they neared the smoke, they saw a line stretched between two trees. On the line, neatly pegged, hung a pair of strangely familiar black and red striped socks.

Beyond the line, by a cheerful wood fire sat Natty Socks, holding a frying-pan, in which frizzled some most appetizing smelling bacon.

'Hello, Natty,' said Mumfie and Scarecrow, coming up. 'I see you are about to have breakfast.' They sniffed hungrily.

'Lunch,' said Natty, without looking up. He poked the bacon with a twig, turning it deftly.

Mumfie and Scarecrow sat down, close to the frying-pan. They eyed it intently.

'I'm hungry,' announced Mumfie longingly. 'Aren't you, Scarecrow? We made such an early start.'

'I certainly am,' said Scarecrow.

'Natty, we have come to talk business, but I think before we begin, we had better have something to eat, don't you?'

The tramp looked up.

'Ho! It's *you*.'

'Yes,' said Mumfie hopefully. 'It's us.'

'Well, I ain't got no more.' He took the bacon out of the pan, put it between two tin plates, and started to fry some bread.

'No more what?' asked Scarecrow. 'You had better fry three pieces while you are about it. It will save time.'

'No more bicycles,' said the tramp.

Scarecrow cut two more slices from the loaf.

'Here you are. We don't want any more bicycles—besides,' he glanced up to the line, '*I* haven't any more socks.'

Natty looked from Scarecrow to the socks, which he regarded with an expression of extreme pride.

'Yus,' he said. 'I washed um.'

'So I see,' grumbled Scarecrow. 'Look out—you're burning the bread.'

He watched hungrily as Natty cracked an egg into the pan.

'Three eggs,' said Scarecrow patiently.

'Why?' asked the tramp.

'I've already told you. We are hungry. We can't talk business while we are empty—can we, Mumfie?'

'Certainly not,' said Mumfie.

'Don't want to talk no business.' But Natty cooked two more eggs, and began ladling them out on to the tin plates. He handed a plate to Mumfie, and the other to Scarecrow; keeping the frying-pan for himself.

'Listen,' said Scarecrow between mouthfuls. 'You like those socks, don't you?'

'Yus,' said the tramp. He regarded them fondly.

'Well, those socks are Business. Those socks are what is called a Deal. Big Business,' he explained for Mumfie's benefit.

'We made a deal with you, out of which *we* got a rather indifferent bicycle, and *you* got those magnificent socks. That's right, isn't it?'

'Yus,' agreed the tramp. 'Only I calls it swops.'

'Oh.' Scarecrow was rather crushed. 'Well, now we want to do another deal with you. We want to buy some more of that Reducing Medicine you sold to the Giant a little while ago. We shall want to place quite a big order.'

'And wot do I get?' asked Natty.

'Wait a bit—I'm coming to that. You can have anything you like—within reason. As you know what you want, and we don't, you had better suggest something.'

'Don't want nuthing,' said the tramp. 'Orl right as I am.'

'Nonsense,' said Mumfie. 'You are not a bit all right. Why, look at your hat! It's full of holes. You might try that to begin with.'

Natty took off his hat and looked at it. He turned it round and round.

'It ain't what you might call helegant, but it keeps me 'ead cool.' He put it back again.

'Well, you could do with a new frying-pan,' suggested Mumfie helpfully.

'Why? This one fries, don't it?'

Mumfie sighed. He and Scarecrow both tried many suggestions, but none of them seemed to interest Natty at all. They were almost reduced to despair, when an idea seemed to dawn on the tramp. A slow smile spread itself across his dirty face.

'A party.' He beamed. 'That's it. A proper party—with an invitation card and all. Many's the time I've looked over the 'edges and watched 'em enjoying of 'emselves—tea on the lawn, and that sort of thing. But they don't ask tramps, they don't. That's wot I wants—and a proper hinvitation, mark you—fancy letters, done in gilt—Requests the pleasure, hetcetera. But I don't suppose you could arrange that?'

'Why, of course!' Mumfie poked Scarecrow. 'We could easily—couldn't we, Scarecrow?'

'Naturally. We will ask him to the house-warming party. Only you'll have to wait a week or so, because the house isn't built yet. As soon as it's ready you can be sure of an invitation. You won't mind waiting, will you?'

'No,' said the tramp. 'But 'ow will I know you will do wot you sez?'

Mumfie looked surprised. 'But of course we will. What does he mean, Scarecrow? What a funny idea.'

'Orl rite—orl rite.' Natty looked at him. 'I'll take your word for it. Probably barmy—but there it is.'

'Then it's a deal?' Scarecrow held out his hand.

'It's a deal, chum.' Natty shook it warmly. ' 'Ave a look in me pack—there's a bottle or two in there.'

'Have you got the recipe?' asked Mumfie anxiously. 'I'm afraid these won't be enough. He needs a bottle at a time you know.'

'Go on!' said the tramp.

'Yes, he does, really. I hope you haven't forgotten how to make it.'

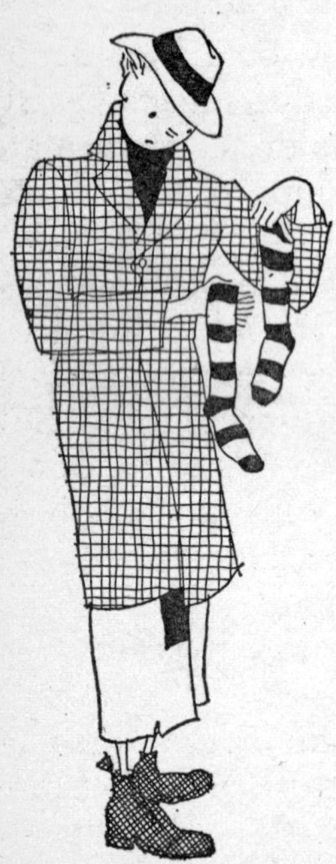

'Not me. It's easy. 'Ere, I'll write it down for you.' He tore off a piece from the paper in which the bacon had been wrapped.

'Got a pencil?'

Mumfie fished in his pocket and found a stump.

'Now, let me see.' He scratched his head, and slowly wrote out the recipe.

'There you are—mind you mixes it up properly. The currant juice is just for colour—folks won't buy unless it looks happetizing like. Just see if me socks is dry, chum. Save me getting up.'

Scarecrow took the socks down from the line. He held them rather regretfully. He put the recipe carefully into Mumfie's pocket, and the two bottles into his own. They said good-bye to Natty, and left him drawing on the socks; a contented expression on his face.

'See you at the party,' called Mumfie, as they went off through the wood.

CHAPTER FOURTEEN

Mumfie swung upon the beautiful new blue gate, and gazed with admiration at the cottage.

'Isn't it lovely?' he sighed. 'We had better put the knocker on the door, Scarecrow, and then I really think everything is finished.'

They went through the gate and up the neatly flagged path, between whose crevices Mumfie had planted tiny rock plants. Triumphantly they nailed a fine brass ship knocker to the door. They went inside to see that everything was ready.

'We had better light the fire,' suggested Scarecrow. 'It will make it look more cosy—besides, it still gets chilly of an evening.'

He lit the fire, while Mumfie went out into the garden—which fortunately had not been much harmed by the fire—and picked a bunch of bright flowers to put on the table. He got a red checked cloth from the drawer, and started to lay for the evening meal. From time to time he looked at his watch.

'I wonder what time they will be arriving?' He jumped up and down excitedly, and whistled to himself a happy tune. 'It's a good thing Uncle Samuel was able to go into the town and fetch them, so that we could get everything ready—supper and all. It smells good, doesn't it, Scarecrow?'

A savoury smell of stew drifted in from the kitchen. Scarecrow had been very busy earlier in the afternoon, peeling onions and potatoes and celery, and cutting a fine cabbage from the garden. Mumfie did not know very much about cooking, but Scarecrow assured him that the best thing you could do with a stew was to put in everything you could find. The result certainly looked very promising, he decided, giving it a stir. He added some more salt, and some herbs; and then came back to watch Mumfie, who was running round the room, a large apron tied round his waist, putting finishing touches here and there

'It's half-past six,' he said. 'Do you think everything looks all right Scarecrow? Oh, dear, I do wish they'd come. I feels so excited.'

'What was that?' Scarecrow went to look out of the window. He thought he could hear people moving through the wood. 'Here they are!' he cried, hastily scrambling out of his apron.

Mumfie ran to the door and flung it wide, as Uncle Samuel came to the gate, carrying a valise in one hand, and various parcels in the other.

Behind him, in a decent black bonnet with roses nodding in front, was Mummy Jumbo—and behind her, in his Sunday suit, and carrying another valise, strode Daddy Jumbo. They stood at the gate, and stared at the cottage as though they could not believe their eyes.

'Well, lawks-a-mussy!' exclaimed Mummy Jumbo, putting her hand up to her mouth. 'Am I dreaming, Papa?'

Then she caught sight of a small, fat figure, who at that moment had flung open the front door.

She dropped all her parcels, and ran through the gate. Mumfie rushed down the path to meet her. He flung himself into her arms.

'Oh, Mama!' cried Mumfie.

'Mumfie, my darling pet,' said his mama, kissing first one round cheek and then the other, not to mention the tips of his ears, and the top of his head.

'Let me look at you, my lamb.' She held him away from her. 'Why, I declare you've grown. He looks well, doesn't he, Pa?'

Mumfie scampered to his papa, who kissed him, and tweaked his left ear.

'Come along.' He dragged them both by the hand. 'Come inside and see everything. Oh, Uncle Samuel—isn't this exciting?'

Scarecrow had been watching this affecting scene through the window

'It must be nice to have a mama and papa to be so fond of you,' he thought.

As the family advanced up the path he suddenly decided that he would go into the kitchen to see how the stew was getting along.

'It isn't even as though I were a relation,' he said to himself.

He was stirring the stew when Mumfie's round, rather surprised face came round the door.

'Oh, there you are,' he cried gaily. 'I couldn't think where you had got to. Come along. Mama and papa are longing to see you.'

Scarecrow wiped his hands on the kitchen towel, and

smoothed down his untidy red hair. He followed Mumfie rather slowly into the sitting room.

Mummy Jumbo had taken off her bonnet, and was warming her hands at the fire. Her face lit up with pleasure.

'Why, this is Scarecrow,' she said, beaming at him. 'Mumfie's letters are always full of you. I don't know how he would have got on without you all this long while, what with all the scrapes he gets himself into.' She put an arm round each of them, and kissed them both heartily.

Papa Jumbo wrung Scarecrow by the hand; Uncle Samuel, who had seated himself in a comfortable chair by the fire, beamed round upon the company.

'What is that savoury smell?' asked Papa Jumbo presently, when he could get a word in through Mumfie's and Scarecrow's chattering.

Scarecrow was feeling completely happy and at

home. He could almost think that at last he had a family of his own, everyone was so kind, and pleased to see him.

'Oh, my goodness!' He broke off. 'That's the stew. I had nearly forgotten about it. I think we had better have supper quite soon, Mumfie—we don't want it to boil away.'

'Here am I sitting talking, and you must all be starving.'

Mummy Jumbo got up and bustled out to the kitchen.

'You run and get ready, dears. I'll dish it up.'

Mumfie and Scarecrow scampered up the stairs to their little bedroom under the eaves. Mumfie had managed to get some of the same rose-and-trellis-patterned wall paper of which he was so fond. The furniture was painted white. There was a lamp with a pink shade, which coloured the room with a rosy glow. On one side of the room was a small square bed with a pink eiderdown; opposite it lay a rather longer bed with a blue eiderdown.

'O-o!' said Mumfie, spluttering in the pink china basin, 'I does feel so happy. Weren't they pleased, Scarecrow?'

'I feel kind of cheerful myself,' said Scarecrow rather gruffly. He whistled a tune to himself.

They ran downstairs, to find the family at table, with Mummy Jumbo ladling out the stew.

'Why, this is excellent,' she said, tasting it; while Scarecrow watched her rather nervously. 'Someone is a very good cook.'

Scarecrow blushed. 'You wait 'til you come to the pudding,' he said. 'Mumfie made the pudding.'

'Oh, he did, did he!' teased Papa Jumbo. 'In that case I'm not having any.'

Mumfie looked at his papa, and giggled.

'All the more for us,' he said cheekily.

He ran out to the kitchen, where he had put in the larder to cool the beautiful chocolate shape which he had made that morning, after carefully reading the instructions on the packet. He eased it away from the edges of the mould, and then turned it out on a dish. It came away with a sucky, plopping sound.

'It's turned out!' sang Mumfie in a pleased voice. He carried it into the sitting-room, an expression of extreme pride on his face.

'Look Mama. It's turned out. I made it all by myself. Didn't I, Scarecrow?'

He helped himself to a good deal of clotted cream, and decided after a while that he was a very good cook.

'When are we going to have the party?' he asked presently, when supper had been cleared away and washed up, and they were all sitting round the fire.

'What's this about a party?' said Papa Jumbo, puffing contentedly at his pipe.

'Oh, we're going to give a lovely party, aren't we, Scarecrow? A house-warming party. Uncle Samuel said he would help us with the invitations, and the rabbits will take them round.'

'I think we should have it on Saturday,' said Uncle Samuel. 'Saturday is a partyish sort of day. You two had better come round in the morning and help me to write the things out. You can come over on the bicycle. I suppose you've a good idea who you want to invite?'

'Oh, yes,' said Mumfie. 'We must invite Natty Socks to begin with. Shall we be able to write the invitations in gilt, Uncle Samuel? He particularly said gilt.'

'Well, we could use gold ink I suppose—nasty messy stuff, and in rather bad taste.'

'Oh, but so is Natty Socks,' said Mumfie happily. 'He will simply love gold ink. Then, of course, we must ask the Giant—I wonder what his name is, Scarecrow?—we never found out—oh, but never mind—we can just address it Mister Giant, he's the only one, so it won't go astray. We can get a wood-pigeon to take the note up, and it can take a bottle of reducing mixture at the same time, otherwise he will never be able to get inside the house. I hope we didn't mix it *too* strong, Scarecrow. Then we must ask the squirrels, and the rabbits, and the wood-cutter and family.' He counted off a list of the guests on his fingers.

'Well,' announced Uncle Samuel, getting up, 'I must be taking myself off now. You young fellows come round in the morning. Good-bye, my dear, very nice to see you home again.' He kissed his sister, and went down to the gate with Papa Jumbo.

'Now, darlings, I think it's time you both went off to bed. You'll want to be fresh for tomorrow.' Mummy Jumbo turned to them.

'Off you go. I'll bring you up some hot cocoa when you're in bed.' She kissed them both.

Mumfie and Scarecrow went upstairs, Mumfie lighting the way with a candle.

Soon they had drunk their cocoa and Mummy Jumbo had tucked them up and kissed them both good night.

Mumfie snuggled comfortably under the warm eiderdown.

He looked across at Scarecrow, whose carroty head was appearing over the blue cover.

'Night-night, Scarecrow.' he said sleepily.

'Night-night,' said Scarecrow, taking a last admiring look at his new blue pyjamas.

'It's nice to be home,' whispered Mumfie into his pillow.

They turned over and nestled down to sleep.

CHAPTER FIFTEEN

Mumfie opened one eye sleepily, and pushed his trunk out from under the bedclothes. He had awoken with an excited feeling inside, as if something pleasant were going to happen today.

'It's Saturday,' he remembered. He burst out of bed, and flew over to the window. Outside, a thrush sang shrilly in the morning sunlight.

Mumfie danced over to Scarecrow's bed and bounced on it. He pulled back the bedclothes.

'Wake up, Scarecrow—it's a lovely day.'

Scarecrow climbed out of bed. Together they danced round the room.

'Isn't it a good thing it is fine? We shall be able to have tea in the garden. I wonder why Uncle Samuel wouldn't let us come with him when he went into town yesterday—he was awfully mysterious about it?'

'I can't imagine,' said Scarecrow. 'Are you ready?'

They spent the morning in numerous preparations for the party. They carried out tables and clipped down the tablecloths, so that they would not flutter in the wind. They rushed continually to the front gate, where tradesmen arrived with their carts, bringing baskets, and panniers, and boxes filled with fresh strawberries, raspberries, lovely sugar cakes and inviting rolls and sandwiches. Uncle Samuel had insisted upon providing for the catering. A party was no fun, he said, if you had to do all the work for it yourself.

After lunch Mummy Jumbo turned them out into the orchard. They lay in the hammock which Papa Jumbo had fixed up for them, swinging idly in the warm, drowsy air.

'I wonder if Natty Socks was excited about his invitation?' said Mumfie. 'I thought the gold looked very fine—and it was fun doing it—in spite of what Uncle Samuel said.'

'So did I,' agreed Scarecrow. 'I expect the Giant will enjoy the party too. The weasels and ferrets and stoats will have been sorry that they behaved so badly, when they saw everyone else's invitations.'

'I shall take care to introduce the Giant to a few beetles,' Mumfie giggled. 'Did you hear what Uncle Samuel said to the fox, Scarecrow?'

'I should just think I did! You could hear it a mile off. *He* won't be around here again in a hurry. Your uncle ended by saying that if he so much as showed his face in the forest again, he would find himself without any face to show another time.'

'Yes, and then he whacked him with his cane, and chased him down the garden path, throwing flowerpots after him.'

Scarecrow roared with laughter at the memory.

'He's a pretty good shot too, is Uncle Samuel. Come on—it's three o'clock. We had better be getting ready.'

They had just changed into their comfortable new playsuits, and were brushed and tidy, when the first guests began to arrive. Soon the garden was filled with laughing and chattering groups, all proffering their congratulations upon the Jumbo family's delightful new house.

Word had gone round that the Giant was expected, and the air was filled with pleasurable anticipation. Few of them had ever seen a giant, and Mumfie and Scarecrow had been careful to lay most of the responsibility for past troubles upon the fox, who was indeed, they thought, mostly to blame with his cunning and greed.

'I do hope he will be careful where he treads, squeaked Hannibal Beetle. 'Look, Mumfie, I've got my new patent-leather boots on. Do you like them?'

'I think they're lovely,' admired Mumfie. 'And you needn't worry about the Giant's being careful. I've given him a very good talking to about beetles, which he won't be likely to forget in a hurry.'

He looked anxiously towards the gate. There had so far been no sign of Natty Socks.

'I wish Natty would hurry up and come,' he said to Scarecrow. 'Wouldn't it be dreadful if he didn't get his invitation?'

'You need not worry.' Scarecrow pointed over the hedge. Through the trees which fringed the clearing shambled Natty. He had certainly taken a good deal of trouble to dress himself up for the party. His head was crowned with a battered top hat. He had put on a collar which, though several sizes too big for him, was quite dazzlingly clean and starched, in contrast to the rest of his appearance. Round his neck was a green knitted tie. A capacious frock coat trailed its tattered hems behind him. He wore yellow cotton gloves, and quite respectable though sturdy boots, over which Scarecrow's socks appeared below the hems of his trousers, which he had turned up, the better to display his pride and joy.

Mumfie rushed to meet him.

'Hullo, Natty.' He caught him by the arm. 'I'm so glad you could come. Come along in.'

' 'Old on a minute.' The tramp fumbled about in his pockets. 'Where is it? 'Ere we are.'

He proudly presented to his small host the invitation card—lettered in gold ink—which Mumfie had so laboriously written out.

'Do you mind if I keeps it?' Natty put it back in his pocket. 'Sort of souvenir, you know—do to put in the family halbum! My, wot a to-do! This is a proper party, this is. When's tea?'

'Ever so soon now.' Mumfie danced round him. 'We are just waiting for the Giant—he should be here any moment now. Come and I'll introduce you to everybody.'

He was busy taking Natty Socks around, when there was a thundering and cracking in the forest. The trees began to sway, and the earth shook. The

guests all stopped what they were about, and looked expectantly towards the clearing. Across the grass strode the Giant. He stopped before the gate and peered down into the garden. Among the crowd of little faces turned up to his, he searched for Uncle Samuel.

'Uncle Samuel?' he said. And his voice, though he tried to speak softly, was so loud that several beetles were temporarily deafened.

'Here I am,' called Uncle Samuel, pushing through the crowd, looking very fine and important in his best check waistcoat.

'But, my dear fellow—hadn't you better take some of the mixture? I'm afraid you will never get in, the way you are.'

'Oh, yes, indeed,' agreed the Giant. 'I just wanted to make sure that I had come to the right house. I didn't want to take it until I got here, it would have been such a terrible long way to walk. But you need not worry—I have been most careful not to tread on anything.'

He sat down in the clearing, while the guests peeped at him over the hedge.

'My!' exclaimed Hannibal Beetle, who had climbed up on to the wall. 'What's he going to do now? Take care, Henrietta,' he warned his sister. 'You'd better not go too close.'

Mumfie pushed open the gate and went out. Amidst murmurs of admiration from the crowd, he climbed up on to the Giant's knee.

'Did you get the medicine all right?' he asked. 'I hope we mixed it properly.'

'Oh, yes, I got it quite safely—oh, and I didn't forget to tip the pigeon. Hold the cup for me while I pour it out.' He pulled a bottle from the pocket of his leather jacket, and handed Mumfie a horn drinking cup. Mumfie held it firmly round the narrowest part,

REDUCING

and watched the Giant pour out the pink coloured mixture.

'I hope it won't taste nasty without the lemonade,' he said.

'Not a bit. It tastes of currants. Well, cheerio!'

The Giant raised the horn and drank from it.

To the accompaniment of a good deal of Oh!-ing and Ah!-ing, together with various other exclamations of astonishment, he grew smaller and smaller, until he stood little more than a head taller than Uncle Samuel.

'Excellent,' said Scarecrow, removing Hannibal from the gate, which he swung open. 'Now come along in, and we'll all have tea. It's a good thing the medicine worked,' he whispered to Mumfie, 'or we should never have been able to feed him.'

A most magnificent tea had been set out upon the tables. Mummy and Daddy Jumbo had the places of honour at the foot and head of the table. Uncle Samuel sat next to the Giant, who had refused to let him out of his sight; Scarecrow and Mumfie sat one on either side of Natty Socks plying him with food, and making sure that he was enjoying himself at his first party.

They watched the Giant with apprehension. From the way in which the food before him was disappearing it would almost seem that though the medicine had been effectual in reducing his person, and his clothes, it had in no way affected his appetite. Scarecrow stretched across the table and tactfully removed a fast diminishing bowl of strawberries.

'Have a strawberry,' he said to Mumfie. 'While there's some left,' he added under his breath.

Mumfie helped himself. He squashed them up with his fork, and mixed them with sugar and cream. He beamed round upon his friends.

After tea they played games, in which the Giant and

Natty joined with great enthusiasm. Uncle Samuel suggested Balloon-ball. He pulled from his pockets dozens of balloons, which he handed to Scarecrow, suggesting that he should blow them up.

'No,' said Scarecrow firmly. 'Not me. I've had enough of that to last me a lifetime. Wait a minute, though.'

He disappeared, and returned with the bicycle-pump, with which he made short work of the balloons.

The Giant and Natty picked up sides. The Giant chose Uncle Samuel, and Natty chose Scarecrow.

There was quite a battle as to who should have Mumfie, but it was finally decided that he and Uncle Samuel could not possibly play on the same side.

It was then that the Giant caught sight of Hannibal Beetle, who was at the time sitting on the grass admiring his new boots.

'You,' called the Giant. 'And the lady next to you.'

Hannibal and Henrietta got up and proudly ranged themselves beside him.

Balloon-ball was an excellent game. Natty removed his top hat, his frock coat, and his ordinary coat, his collar and smart green tie. He flung himself into the fray.

'Goodness!' exclaimed a rabbit. 'You do wear a lot.'

'Me entire wardrobe,' said Natty with dignity. 'Who's going to referee this 'ere game?'

Papa Jumbo stepped into the field with a large silver whistle on which he blew repeatedly.

The object of the game was to burst the other side's balloons, which were distinguished by a different colour. Scarecrow was very good at this—he had had a good deal of practice.

As the evening drew in, Mama Jumbo lighted lanterns which she had hung from the trees. Mumfie thought how pretty they looked as he sat down to get his breath after the game, which had ended in a draw.

He watched with appreciation as a wonderful iced pudding appeared, together with other dainties of a cool and refreshing nature.

The Giant sat on the grass, talking happily to those around him. Uncle Samuel was discoursing to him on the rival merits of stilton and gorgonzola cheese, when he noticed that his friend seemed to be taking up rather more room than when had sat down.

'He's probably overeaten,' he said to himself.

But no; the Giant was certainly getting bigger.

'I say, old chap!' He nudged him. 'Have you got any more of that stuff on you?'

'Why, no. Oh, dear—am I growing again?'

'I am very much afraid so.'

'Then in that case I had better get outside the garden. But first of all I want to make a speech.'

'Why, certainly, my dear chap.' Uncle Samuel got up. 'Pray silence for our honoured guest. He wants to make a speech.'

The rapidly growing giant got up and went to the head of the table. All heads were turned to him as he began.

'Ladies and Gentlemen—and Beetles. Ahem! Oh, dear, I'm not much good at this—you come and stand by me, Uncle Samuel, in case I run down.'

Mumfie and Scarecrow looked from the speaker to the table, on which were arranged some very inviting looking parcels.

'Well—it's like this.' The Giant began again. 'Me and Uncle Samuel got together, and we decided as this was a very special occasion, it ought to be celebrated with——'

'Leave that part until last,' interrupted Uncle Samuel. 'That bit comes at the end.'

'Oh, yes—of course. Well, I'm afraid that I have been a very bad giant, and I want to apologize to everybody for all the trouble I've caused. I hope no one is angry with me any more?' He looked round hopefully.

There were cries of appreciation and encouragement from all sides.

'I would like to say how much I have enjoyed this party, and all the good food, and interesting conversation. Perhaps you will let me come down again sometimes and visit you, now that I have this wonderful medicine. You've no idea how lonely I've been . . .'

Uncle Samuel coughed loudly. 'Don't talk about yourself so much,' he whispered.

'Oh, no—of course—oh, dear, I'm getting awfully big. I think you had better go on, Uncle Samuel—I'll listen from the other side of the hedge.'

Amid enthusiastic applause, he removed himself from the garden, and sat down ouside. He felt something tickling his elbow.

'Hullo!' said Hannibal and Henrietta Beetle. 'We've come to keep you company, so that you won't feel out of things.' The Giant was quite overcome by their kindness; his face shone with emotion.

But Uncle Samuel had risen behind the table. He took a sip of lemonade, and paused to cut himself a slice of cucumber peel, which he clapped across his forehead. He cleared his throat and began.

'Here we are, sitting in the garden of a very fine new cottage.' He waved his hand with a grand gesture. 'I am sure you have all enjoyed yourselves. We can more or less take that for granted. But have you paused to consider whom we have to thank for all this merriment and jollification? Why, my nephew Mumfie, and his friend Scarecrow!'

His words were greeted with storms of applause. It

became necessary to ask the Giant to refrain from clapping as the noise was really deafening.

When quiet had been obtained, Uncle Samuel continued.

'The Giant and I got together, and decided that a small token of our appreciation would not come amiss. Come up here, Mumfie and Scarecrow, will you?'

Mumfie and Scarecrow ran up to the table. They stood waiting expectantly, as Uncle Samuel put his spectacles on his nose and peered at the labels on the parcels.

'Mumfie—this is for you—hold it carefully, and don't drop it.'

Mumfie took hold of the bright wicker basket, and felt something rustle inside it. His heart thundering with excitement, he set the basket down, and opened it.

Out tumbled a small, round puppy, which bumbled over to him, falling over its own feet, and sticking out its tiny sharp claws in frantic efforts to bite the buttons on his suit. Mumfie was quite speechless with delight. He picked up the puppy and hugged it to him.

Uncle Samuel and the Giant exchanged pleased glances.

'We thought,' said Uncle Samuel, 'that now you have come home again you would like a dog to go about with you. But for heaven's sake, don't overfeed it. And now we come to Scarecrow—who, if I may say so—is just the sort of fellow I should choose to have alongside me in a shipwreck.'

He wheeled from behind the table, where it had stood hidden under a cloth, a beautiful, shining motor-bicycle.

Scarecrow's eyes nearly fell out of his head. He looked from the bicycle to Uncle Samuel.

'For *me*?' he said.

He stood still for a moment, and then let out a wild yell, and went rushing round and round the garden, turning cartwheels and somersaults, until Mumfie wondered whether the shock had not been too much for him.

Then he came and sat astride the bicycle, gazing at it, as if he could not believe his eyes. Uncle Samuel waved aside their thanks.

'Now we come to Natty—who has been so helpful with his Giant Reducing Mixture.'

He took a parcel from the table and handed it to Natty, who upon hearing his name had shuffled forward. Inside the parcel was a fine black and red striped jersey, which went very well with a certain pair of socks. Natty held it up to the light and inspected it.

'Why—it's NEW!' he gasped. He took off his coats, and proceeded to put it on, amid loud cheering. With mumbled thanks, he swaggered back to his place and sat down.

'This is a *proper* party,' he said with satisfaction. 'First time I ever 'ad anything new in me life,' he confided to his neighbour.

Uncle Samuel left the table, and went over to the gate. 'Here is something for you, too.' He presented a box to the Giant.

'What—a present for me?—Oh, I must say—this *is* kind.'

He fumbled with the string, ably assisted by Henrietta and Hannibal.

'Why, it's a set of chessmen!'

'Yes,' said Uncle Samuel. 'Those are to be used when you come to stay with me. I hope that in future we shall have many games together.'

'Oh, but how very kind. I *shall* look forward to that. My goodness, but I don't know when I have enjoyed myself so much. So much good company—and now this delightful present. Mind, Hannibal.'

He gently removed the beetle, and felt in his pocket.

'I didn't forget you, either. Will you please accept this small token of my affection and regard?'

Uncle Samuel, fixing his spectacles more securely on his nose, peered at the label on the wooden crate, which the Giant had fetched from his pocket.

'Jamaica Rum,' he read out. 'Well! well! well! I call that very thoughtful of you, my dear fellow—very thoughtful indeed.' He regarded the crate with considerable satisfaction.

Mumfie had been watching this scene with the puppy in his arms. He put it down and went over to Scarecrow, who was still sitting on the bicycle.

'I've got something for you, too,' he said. 'Here you are.'

'Why—socks!' exclaimed Scarecrow, unwrapping

them, and holding them up. 'Oh, Mumfie, how very thoughtful of you.'

'I hope you like them. I got Uncle Samuel to choose them for me when he went into town yesterday.'

Scarecrow took off his boots and put on the new socks, which were bright red and blue. He held out his feet, admiring them.

'They are lovely, Mumfie. Thank you ever so much. Here's something for you, too—it's not very much—but I hope you will like it—I made it myself.'

'Look,' said Mumfie to the puppy, showing it the gay, painted boat which Scarecrow had carved from soft wood. 'Isn't it lovely? You are clever, Scarecrow. I shall sail it in the rhododendron pond, when next we go to visit Uncle Samuel. Now let's go and thank the Giant.'

He picked up his puppy and went out of the gate.

'I do love him,' he said, holding the wriggling little creature out for the Giant's inspection. 'I wonder what I shall call it?'

'Why not call it Hannibal, after me,' shrilled Hannibal Beetle

'Certainly not,' said Scarecrow severely. 'Don't be so conceited, Hannibal.'

'Oh, dear.' The Giant sighed. 'That rather puts the stopper on the suggestion that I was about to make.'

'What was that?' asked Mumfie interestedly.

'Well, I was going to suggest that you named it after me.'

'I think that is a very good plan—but I don't know what your name is!'

'Ferdinand Ulric Bartholomew Silas Yogel,' said the Giant. 'You can choose whichever name you wish.'

'Oh,' said Mumfie. 'Oh, dear, that is a very long name. I don't think I could ever remember it.'

'F. U. B. S. Yogel,' repeated the Giant. 'Here, you can see it on my name-tape.'

He showed Mumfie the corner of his handkerchief, in which was sewn a neatly printed tape.

Mumfie spelt out the initials. 'F.U.B.S.Y. Fubsy! That's it, I shall just call him by your initials. Only I shall spell it Fubsie, because it looks more comfortable.'

'A splendid idea,' agreed the Giant. 'Well, now, I really must be going. I don't know when I have spent such a pleasant evening. Can I give anybody a lift?'

'Yes, please,' squeaked Hannibal and Henrietta.

'Oh, don't bother about us, we'll just stay where we are.'

They popped their heads back into a leather pocket. This was a sign for people to begin taking their leave. They thanked their hosts and hostess, saying what a wonderful party it had been. Many availed themselves of the Giant's kind offer of a lift. They scrambled all over him—into his pockets and up his coat-sleeves; one or two adventurous rabbits even went so far as to climb on to his head. They snuggled down into his curly red hair. When everybody was comfortably settled, the Giant waved good-bye, and strode off into the forest.

Mumfie and Scarecrow watched him until he disappeared between the trees, his head among the topmost branches. Then they turned to Uncle Samuel, who was standing in the path, saying good night to Mummy and Daddy Jumbo.

'It *has* been a lovely party,' they said. 'May we go a little way with Uncle Samuel, Mama?' asked Mumfie.

They trotted along beside him until they came to the rowan bush.

'Now, then, back you go,' he said. He patted them both on the head, and wished them good night.

They turned again towards the house, Fubsie the puppy bumbling beside them.

Through the trees they could see the lights from the cottage windows beaming at them in a friendly and welcoming manner. They could hear Mummy Jumbo singing a little song to herself as she busied herself about Papa Jumbo's supper.

She came to the front door, her comfortable form outlined against the light. She looked down the path, shading her eyes with her hand.

'Oh, there you are, dears,' she called out.

Mumfie and Scarecrow ran up the path towards her.

She put an arm round each of them, and drew them into the house.

THE END

THE HOW AND WHY BOOK OF WILD ANIMALS 40p

552 86508 7

Information about many of the world's most interesting wild animals, what they look like, where they live, how they hunt, what they eat, their intelligence and means of protection—these are some of the features that make this book both educational and entertaining.

THE ADVENTURES OF ODD AND ELSEWHERE
by JAMES ROOSE-EVANS 25p

552 52038 Carousel Fiction

Sprawled in a corner, the small bear could see the removal van drive away. Everybody had gone and Odd was left alone in the house. But Odd was not alone for long. Hanging upside down by one leg in a tall cupboard was a circus clown—Elsewhere.

Odd and Elsewhere went to live next door—in Fenton House owned by the National Trust—with Collander Moll, the caretaker, and her father Hallelujah Jones, a retired Welsh policeman, who did the garden. One day they went off exploring—and that was the start of all their adventures.

HOKE'S JOKES, CARTOONS AND FUNNY THINGS
by HELEN HOKE 20p

552 54063 3 Carousel Non-Fiction

Every page of this book is packed with colourful cartoons, jokes and riddles.

MALCOLM SAVILLE'S COUNTRY BOOK 30p

552 54030 7 Carousel Non-Fiction

It is not necessary to go far into the countryside to find a whole new world awaiting exploration. Malcolm Saville tells you how to gain the most from a day at the farm, a quiet browse by a pond, or a stroll along the hedgerows or through a wood—and stresses that there is much to be found all the year round.

He also tells you how to recognize the wild flowers and trees of the countryside. You will discover how much extra enjoyment can be had on a walk by using a compass or a map, how to picnic and how to camp, and even how to recognize the stars at night.

If you would like to receive a newsletter telling you about our new children's books, fill in the coupon with your name and address and send it to:

Gillian Osband,
Transworld Publishers Ltd,
Century House,
61–63, Uxbridge Road,
London, W.5.

NAME ....

ADDRESS ....

....

....

CHILDREN'S NEWSLETTER

All these books are available at your bookshop or can be ordered direct from Transworld Publishers Ltd., Cash Sales Dept., P.O. Box 11, Falmouth, Cornwall.
Please send full name and address together with cheque or postal order—no currency, and allow 10p per book to cover postage and packing (plus 5p each for additional copies).